MW00473554

SEEING BEAUTY

and SAYING

BEAUTIFULLY

THE SWANS ARE NOT SILENT

Book Six

SEEING BEAUTY
and SAYING
BEAUTIFULLY

The Power of Poetic Effort in the Work of
GEORGE HERBERT, GEORGE WHITEFIELD, AND C. S. LEWIS

JOHN PIPER

WHEATON, ILLINOIS

Seeing Beauty and Saying Beautifully

Copyright © 2014 by Desiring God Foundation

Published by Crossway
1300 Crescent Street
Wheaton, Illinois 60187

Cover design: Dual Identity, inc.

Cover portrait illustrations: Howell Golson

Cover image: Shutterstock

First printing 2014

Printed in the United States of America

Trade paperback ISBN: 978-1-4335-4294-7
ePub ISBN: 978-1-4335-4297-8
PDF ISBN: 978-1-4335-4295-4
Mobipocket ISBN: 978-1-4335-4296-1

Library of Congress Cataloging-in-Publication Data
Piper, John, 1946–
    Seeing beauty and saying beautifully : the power of poetic
effort in the work of George Herbert, George Whitefield,
and C.S. Lewis / John Piper.
        pages cm. — (The swans are not silent ; Book 6)
    Includes bibliographical references and index.
    ISBN 978-1-4335-4294-7 (hc)
    1. Christianity and the arts. 2. Creation (Literary, artistic,
etc.)—Religious aspects—Christianity. 3. Aesthetics—
Religious aspects—Christianity. 4. Herbert, George,
1593–1633. 5. Whitefield, George, 1714–1770. 6. Lewis,
C. S. (Clive Staples), 1898–1963. I. Title.
BR115.A8P56   2014
261.5'8—dc23   2013043737

Crossway is a publishing ministry of Good News Publishers.

LB		24	23	22	21	20	19	18	17	16	15	14
15	14	13	12	11	10	9	8	7	6	5	4	3	2	1

In memory of
Clyde S. Kilby
whose classroom poetic effort
made us savor what he saw

CONTENTS

PREFACE

When Eraclius, the successor to Augustine as bishop of Hippo in AD 400, said of his awe-inspiring predecessor, "The swan is silent," he compared his own voice to Augustine's as a chirping cricket. He was not referring mainly to the beauty of Augustine's eloquence but to the beauty and power and fullness of his ideas.

But when I say of George Herbert and George Whitefield and C. S. Lewis that these swans are not silent, I have in mind precisely the way their eloquence and their ideas relate to each other. The aim of this volume of The Swans Are Not Silent is to probe the interrelationship between seeing beauty and saying it beautifully.

GEORGE HERBERT, PASTOR-POET

George Herbert died in 1633 just short of his fortieth birthday. Late in that short life, he became an Anglican country pastor. He wrote a book called *The Country Parson*. But, he is known today because of his peerless combination of poetic craftsmanship and profound Christian faith. If any swan should be considered when pondering the relationship between seeing the beauty of Christ and saying it with unparalleled technical, artistic skill, it is George Herbert. He is "arguably the most skillful and important British devotional lyricist of [the seventeenth century] or any other time."[1]

---

[1] "George Herbert," *Poetry Foundation*, accessed February 21, 2014, http://www.poetryfoundation.org/bio/george-herbert.

GEORGE WHITEFIELD, PREACHER-DRAMATIST

George Whitefield was an English Christian evangelist who lived from 1714 to 1770. He crossed the Atlantic thirteen times and is buried, not in his homeland, but in Newburyport, Massachusetts. Along with John Wesley in England, Howell Harris in Wales, and Jonathan Edwards in America—but more international than any of them—Whitefield was a primary catalyst of the First Great Awakening.

The preaching pace he set for thirty years was almost superhuman. Sober estimates are that he spoke about one thousand times every year for thirty years. That included at least eighteen thousand sermons and twelve thousand talks and exhortations.[2] But it is not the pace that concerns us in this book, but the power—specifically the connections between the power of his biblical perception, the power of his natural eloquence, and the power of his spiritual effectiveness.

Jonathan Edwards's wife Sarah said that Whitefield was a "born orator."[3] Benjamin Franklin, who rejected Whitefield's entire theology, said, "Every accent, every emphasis, every modulation of voice, was so perfectly well turned, and well-placed, that without being interested in the subject, one could not help being pleased with the discourse."[4] So people have asked, "Was, then, Whitefield's effectiveness only natural rather than spiritual and eternal?" J. C. Ryle certainly did not think so: "I believe that the direct good which he did to immortal souls was enormous. I will go further—I believe it is incalculable."[5]

George Whitefield was not a poet in the strict sense the way George Herbert was. But his preaching craft, with all its verbal and emotional and physical dimensions, was such a work of art that Benjamin Franklin said that listening was "a pleasure of much the same kind with that received from an excellent piece of music."[6] Therefore, Whitefield provides us with a second historical seedbed for our question about the relationship between seeing beauty and saying beautifully.

---

[2] Michael A. G. Haykin, ed., *The Revived Puritan: The Spirituality of George Whitefield* (Dundas, Ontario: Joshua, 2000), 32–33. Arnold Dallimore, *George Whitefield: The Life and Times of the Great Evangelist of the Eighteenth-Century Revival*, (Edinburgh: Banner of Truth, 1970), 2:522.

[3] Haykin, *Revived Puritan*, 35–37.

[4] Harry S. Stout, *The Divine Dramatist: George Whitefield and the Rise of Modern Evangelicalism* (Grand Rapids, MI: Eerdmans, 1991), 204.

[5] J. C. Ryle, *Select Sermons of George Whitefield with an Account of his Life* (Edinburgh: Banner of Truth, 1958), 28.

[6] Stout, *Divine Dramatist*, 204.

C. S. LEWIS, SCHOLAR-NOVELIST

C. S. Lewis is the third focus of our study. Peter Kreeft stands in awe of Lewis and says, "Clive Staples Lewis was not a man: he was a world."[7] Lewis lived from 1898 to 1963 and spent his working life as a professor of Medieval and Renaissance Literature at Oxford and Cambridge. But he is known most widely as the author of the children's books (which adults love) The Chronicles of Narnia, some of which have been made into movies.[8]

Lewis wanted to be a great poet. But he admits at age fifty-six that his poetry met "with little success."[9] Nevertheless, he says,

> The imaginative man in me is . . . continuously operative. . . . It was he . . . who led me to embody my religious belief in symbolical . . . forms, ranging from Screwtape to a kind of theologized science-fiction. And it was of course he who has brought me, in the last few years, to write the series of Narnian stories for children.[10]

This "imaginative man" who wanted to be a great poet remained a real poet in all his prose. Alister McGrath expressed it well when he said that much of Lewis's power was

> His ability to write prose tinged with a poetic vision, its carefully crafted phrases lingering in the memory because they have captivated the imagination. The qualities we associate with good poetry . . . [abound] in Lewis's prose.[11]

Lewis had the eyes and the pen of a poet. Of all the people I have ever read, Lewis—like Jonathan Edwards, but for different reasons—sees beauty and wonder in what he looks at, and awakens my mind to do the same. He saw beauty, and what he saw, he said beautifully. The combination has given him lasting power. He is the most widely read twentieth-century apologist today. He is more popular and influential now than he ever was in his lifetime.

---

[7] Peter Kreeft, *C. S. Lewis: A Critical Essay* (Grand Rapids, MI: Eerdmans, 1969), 4.
[8] Most recently, *The Lion, the Witch, and the Wardrobe* (2005), *Prince Caspian* (2008), and *The Voyage of the Dawn Treader* (2010).
[9] Walter Hooper, ed., *The Collected Letters of C. S. Lewis: Narnia, Cambridge, and Joy, 1950–1963*, vol. 3 (San Francisco: HarperCollins, 2007), 517.
[10] Ibid.
[11] Alister McGrath, *C. S. Lewis–A Life: Eccentric Genius, Reluctant Prophet* (Carol Stream, IL: Tyndale, 2013), 108.

THREE ANGLICANS AND THEIR POETIC EFFORT

This is a book about the interrelationship between seeing beauty and saying it beautifully—and the impact that the effort has on our lives. It is rooted in the life and work of three Anglican Christians—a pastor-poet, a preacher-dramatist, and a scholar-novelist. All of them, in their own ways, made sustained poetic effort in what they spoke and wrote. This book is about that effort and how it relates to seeing beauty and awakening others to see it—especially the beauty of Jesus Christ.

ACKNOWLEDGMENTS

John Donne is usually acknowledged to be the greatest of the so-called metaphysical poets. He was twenty-one years older than George Herbert, and a close friend of Herbert's mother. Donne's influence on Herbert was significant. Some of his most famous lines are:

> No man is an island,
> Entire of itself,
> Every man is a piece of the continent,
> A part of the main. . . .

> And therefore never send to know for whom the bell tolls;
> It tolls for thee.[1]

The older I get and the more of my life on this earth is behind me rather than before me, the more I feel the truth of this. I am what I am as a thread in a fabric, a grape in a cluster, a spark in a fire, a bee in a hive, a nerve in a body, an ingredient in a recipe, a stone in a wall, or a drop in an ocean.

To be sure, I deeply value individuality, and loathe the horrors of constrained, homogenous, communistic sameness. God made individuals with stunning distinctiveness and as absolutely unique refractions of his glory. Nevertheless, the greatest glory is when these refractions compose a unified display of God's greatness, as a stained glass window with thousands of fragments reveals one bright picture—not *in spite of* the differences among the fragments, but *because* of

[1]John Donne, "Meditation 17" (1623) in *The Complete Poetry and Selected Prose of John Donne*, ed. Charles M. Coffin (New York: Random House, 1952), 440–41.

them. Or like a tapestry with millions of matchless threads—yellow, orange, blue, and crimson fragmentary alone—being woven into a perfect whole.

So it is no artificial humility for me to say that I am more thankful at age sixty-eight than I have ever been for the people who have made this book possible. They are more than I can remember or honor. Dozens of those who have made this book possible are dead. They have been dead for centuries and are as much a part of my life as many of the living. In my home, and in high school, and college, and seminary, and graduate school, and college teaching, and pastoring there have been hundreds of people who have shaped the way I think and the way I respond to the world and to God.

And there are the obvious ones who are close and precious. My wife and children and even grandchildren shape my heart in these days. Noël and Talitha make a home for me as the three of us eat and sleep and talk and read and pray together.

David Mathis, the executive editor at desiringGod.org, and Marshall Segal, my executive assistant, protect, distill, provide, suggest, correct, refine, and encourage with devotion and excellence so that I can flourish in the ministry of the Word.

Since stepping down as pastor for preaching at Bethlehem Baptist Church in March of 2013, Desiring God has been my new base of operations. I'm called founder and teacher. They pay my salary. They share me with Bethlehem College and Seminary so that I can function as chancellor and teach part time. All this means that I am surrounded and sustained by an amazing team of partners (at DG and BCS) committed to spreading a passion for the supremacy of God in all things for the joy of all peoples through Jesus Christ.

I thank God for this beautiful fabric of life into which I have been woven.

Crossway has again been willing to publish another volume, this one the sixth, in the series The Swans Are Not Silent. Because of this partnership, the fruit of all the other influences of my life are made available to the public. May God continue to weave, with this book, tens of thousands of threads into the great tapestry of his Christ-exalting purpose in the world.

I am not an island. When the bell tolls for a thousand losses in the lives of others, it tolls for me. And with this book, even more of us will be woven together. The tapestry grows, the beauties increase, and the sorrows multiply—until the last stitch is made and all is beauty.

Christ did not send me to baptize but to preach the gospel, and not with words of eloquent wisdom, lest the cross of Christ be emptied of its power. For the word of the cross is folly to those who are perishing, but to us who are being saved it is the power of God. . . . Where is the debater of this age? Has not God made foolish the wisdom of the world? . . .

For the foolishness of God is wiser than men, and the weakness of God is stronger than men. . . . And I, when I came to you, brothers, did not come proclaiming to you the testimony of God with lofty speech or wisdom. For I decided to know nothing among you except Jesus Christ and him crucified.

The Apostle Paul

1 Corinthians 1:17–2:2

"NOT WITH LOFTY SPEECH OR WISDOM"

Does the Bible Warrant Poetic Effort?

This book is about the relationship between *poetic effort*, on the one hand, and perceiving, relishing, and portraying truth and beauty, on the other hand—especially the truth and beauty of God in Christ. By *poetic effort*, I don't mean the effort to write poetry. Those who make the greatest poetic effort, as I am using the term, may never write a poem. Only one of the three men in this book is known mainly for his poetry—George Herbert. But all three of them made poetic effort in their Christ-exalting communications. They made poetic effort to *see* and *savor* and *show* the glories of Christ. This effort was the God-dependent intention and exertion to find striking, penetrating, imaginative, and awakening ways of expressing the excellencies they saw. My thesis is that this effort to say beautifully is, perhaps surprisingly, a way of seeing and savoring beauty.

For example, when I hear my daughter singing worship songs in her bedroom, my heart is glad. But when I make the effort to put into suitable words what I love about her song—in a conversation, in a birthday card, in a poem—I hear more, see more, love more. This is how it is with all truth and beauty—the wonders of nature, the stunning turns of redemptive history, and the glories of Christ. In making the poetic effort to find fitting words for these wonders, we see and savor them more deeply and speak them with more power. George Herbert, George Whitefield, and C. S. Lewis discovered this long before I did. It has been a profound joy to follow their discovery and use of poetic effort—for Christ and his kingdom.

MY BIGGEST FEAR

My biggest fear in writing this book is that I might contradict the apostle Paul when he says, "Christ did not send me . . . to preach the gospel . . . *with words of eloquent wisdom*, lest the cross of Christ be emptied of its power" (1 Corinthians 1:17),[1] or when he said, "I . . . did not come proclaiming to you the testimony of God *with lofty speech or wisdom*" (1 Corinthians 2:1).[2] There is a way to speak the gospel—a way of eloquence or cleverness or human wisdom—that nullifies the cross of Christ.

James Denney said, "No man can give the impression that he himself is clever and that Christ is mighty to save."[3] This statement has been my constant companion for the last three decades. I long to show that Christ is mighty to save. I dread nullifying the cross. Therefore, the implicit exhortation throughout this book—to make poetic effort and to find striking ways to speak truth—runs the risk of contradicting Scripture. That is a fearful thing.

INDISPENSABLE WORDS

But the risk is unavoidable. Every person who seeks to commend Christ with words faces this issue. And we cannot do without words in commending Christ. We know him in the words of Scripture, and the Scriptures themselves teach us how indispensable words are in the Christian life. God has designed the world and human beings in such a way that his ultimate and highest aims for humanity come about through human words. For example,

---

[1] The NIV 1984 translates 1 Corinthians 1:17, "Not with words of human wisdom"; the NASB, "Not in cleverness of speech"; and the KJV, "Not with wisdom of words."
[2] The NIV translates 1 Corinthians 2:1, "I did not come with *eloquence or human wisdom*"; the NASB, "I did not come with *superiority of speech or of wisdom*"; and the KJV, "[I] came not with *excellency of speech or of wisdom*."
[3] James Denney quoted in John Stott, *Between Two Worlds: The Art of Preaching in the Twentieth Century* (Grand Rapids, MI: Eerdmans, 1982), 325.

- The *new birth* comes about through words (1 Peter 1:23–25): "You have been born again . . . through the living and abiding word of God. . . . This word is the good news that was preached to you" (also, James 1:18).
- Saving *faith* comes about through words (Romans 10:17): "Faith comes from hearing, and hearing through the word of Christ."
- The grace of *edification* comes through words (Ephesians 4:29): "[Let only speech come from your mouth] as fits the occasion, that it may give grace to those who hear."
- Christian *love* and purity of heart and a good conscience come through words (1 Timothy 1:5): "The aim of our charge [our words] is love that issues from a pure heart and a good conscience and a sincere faith."
- The *joy* of Christ in the believer comes through words (John 15:11): "These things I have spoken to you, that my joy may be in you, and that your joy may be full."
- *Freedom* from the power of sin comes through words (John 8:32): "You will know the truth, and the truth will set you free."
- That is, *sanctification* comes through words (John 17:17): "Sanctify them in the truth; your word is truth."
- And final *salvation* comes though teaching with words (1 Timothy 4:16): "Keep a close watch . . . on the teaching. Persist in this, for by so doing you will save both yourself and your hearers."

GOD'S DECISIVE WORK

Of course, if that's all we said about the cause of these great accomplishments (new birth, faith, love, holiness, and salvation), then one might be tempted to think that our giftedness in using words effectively is decisive in bringing these things about. Poetic effort and "wordsmithing" would be paramount. But in fact, our words are not decisive in producing any of these glorious effects. God is.

- *God* made his people alive while they were dead in their sins (Ephesians 2:5), so that they could even hear the words of the gospel.
- By the grace *of God*, our people come to have faith, "This is not [their] own doing; it is the gift of God" (Ephesians 2:8).

- When our people achieve any measure of holiness, it is God "working in [them] that which is pleasing in his sight" (Hebrews 13:21).
- If they experience any Christ-honoring love or joy or peace, it is the fruit of God's Spirit (Galatians 5:22).
- If they fight successfully against any sin, it is "by [God's] Spirit" that they put to death the deeds of the body (Romans 8:13).
- And if they are saved in the end, it is decisively because God "saved [them] . . . not because of [their] works but because of his own purpose and grace" (2 Timothy 1:9). God kept them from stumbling (Jude 1:24); God completed the work that he began (Philippians 1:6).

In other words, all the highest aims of language are decisively the work of God. They are decisively supernatural. And no amount of poetic effort or expertise in the use of words can bring about the great aims of life if God withholds his saving power. Which raises the question: Does, then, the way we use words—does poetic effort—make any difference in whether the great aims of life are achieved?

The Importance of How We Use Words

The New Testament answers yes, at least in regard to the clarity of the words and the attitude of their delivery. The *clarity* of the words matters: "Pray also for us . . . that I may make it *clear*, which is how I ought to speak" (Colossians 4:3–4). "If with your tongue you utter speech that is not intelligible, how will anyone know what is said? For you will be speaking into the air . . ." (1 Corinthians 14:9, cf. v. 19). And the *attitude* of the delivery matters. Paul pleads for prayer, "that words may be given to me in opening my mouth *boldly* to proclaim the mystery of the gospel . . . as I ought to speak" (Ephesians 6:18–20).

This leaves us asking: If God is the decisive cause of the aims of our ministry, and yet God wills that the *clarity* and *attitude* of our words make a difference in their effectiveness, are there other aspects of language (besides clarity and attitude) that might make a difference in their effectiveness? What about poetic effort? What about the effort to find words and ways of putting them together that is surprising and striking and provocative and awakening and creative and imaginative?

UNAVOIDABLE CHOICES OF WORDS

We are not forcing this question on the text of Scripture. It is not we but God who has made words indispensable for the greatest events of the world—spiritual events with eternal effects. And we cannot just quote Scripture. We must talk about it. Explain it. Exult in it. Defend it. Commend it. Herald it. Pray it. And each time we must choose words. Which words will we choose?

We know that different words have different associations and connotations and effects. We must choose how to put these words together in sentences and paragraphs. We must choose how to say them: softly or loudly, quickly or slowly, pausing or not pausing, tenderly or toughly, emotionally or dispassionately, joyfully or sadly, with gestures or without gestures, walking or standing still, smiling or frowning, looking people in the eye or looking past them. We cannot escape this. We must make these choices. We either do it consciously or unconsciously.

FORWARD WITH THE RISK

So I don't take this risk of writing this book because I want to, but because I have had to make these choices every day of my Christian life. Of course, I don't have to write a book about it. But is not writing a book less of a risk? Should I make these choices without reflection? Should I make them without Christian models to help me—like Herbert and Whitefield and Lewis? Should I do the hard work of thinking about these things but not share it with anyone? It seems to me that the risk of each of those options is greater than the risk of writing this book.

So we ask: Did the apostle Paul in 1 Corinthians 1 and 2 intend to discourage all poetic effort in commending the truth and beauty of God in Christ? Did he mean that we should make no prayerful, Bible-guided, God-dependent exertion to find striking, penetrating, imaginative, awakening ways of expressing the excellencies of Christ? I don't think so.[4] And I have six reasons. The most important is the context

---

[4] In the following paragraphs, I am drawing heavily on my chapter "Is There Christian Eloquence: Clear Words and the Wonder of the Cross," in *The Power of Words and the Wonder of God*, ed. John Piper and Justin Taylor (Wheaton, IL: Crossway, 2008), 67–80.

of 1 Corinthians itself and what kind of eloquence Paul actually meant to condemn.

1. WHAT KIND OF ELOQUENCE DID PAUL ACTUALLY CONDEMN?

Let's make our way back into Paul's mind through a recent book on eloquence by Denis Donoghue, professor of English and American Letters at New York University. In his book *On Eloquence*, he argues that eloquence is a surprising, impacting style that is an end in itself.

> A speech or an essay may be eloquent, but if it is, the eloquence is incidental to its aim. Eloquence, as distinct from rhetoric, has no aim: it is a play of words or other expressive means. . . . The main attribute of eloquence is gratuitousness.[5]

> Eloquence does not serve a purpose or an end in action. . . . In rhetoric, one is trying to persuade someone to do something: in eloquence, one is discovering with delight the expressive resources of the means at hand.[6]

I doubt that most people would agree with that definition of eloquence, as if eloquence cannot intentionally stand in the service of a great aim—say the eloquence of Martin Luther King Jr. in the cause of civil rights, or the eloquence of Winston Churchill in the cause of British national defense. But here is why Donoghue's view is important.

The Sophists in Corinth

It expresses the view that was probably behind the "eloquence" in Corinth that Paul wanted no part of. Donoghue agrees with E. M. Cioran that this notion of gratuitous eloquence began with the sophists two thousand years ago.

> The sophists were the first to occupy themselves with a meditation upon words, their value, propriety, and function in the conduct of

---

[5] Denis Donoghue, *On Eloquence* (New Haven, CT: Yale University Press, 2008), 3.
[6] Ibid., 148.

reasoning: the capital step toward *the discovery of style, conceived as a goal in itself, as an intrinsic end*, was taken [by the sophists].[7]

One of the most compelling books on the background of Paul's words about eloquence in 1 Corinthians is Bruce Winter's *Philo and Paul among the Sophists*. Winter's argument is that it is precisely the sophists, and their view of eloquence, that form the backdrop of what Paul says about his own speech and how he ministered in Corinth.[8]

So let's consider briefly Paul's words in 1 Corinthians to see if he gives us enough clues to show what sort of eloquence he is rejecting. Given my definition of poetic effort (which I would call a kind of eloquence), it is clear to me that in the very act of rejecting Greek eloquence, Paul is making poetic effort. For example, in 1 Corinthians 1:25, he says, "The foolishness of God is wiser than men, and the weakness of God is stronger than men." He cannot be unconscious that it is shocking to say that the gospel is "the foolishness of God" and "the weakness of God." This risks blasphemy. He could have spared us preachers the work of explaining this daring, over-the-top description of God's greatest work as foolish and weak. But no! He chose a shocking way to say it. He used irony. He made an effort to select words that would make an impact and force people to wake up and think. That is what I mean by poetic effort. And Paul does it while condemning a certain kind of "eloquence."

---

[7] Ibid., 136 (emphasis added).

[8] "The wise, the well born and the powerful epitomized the class from which the sophists came and which the latter helped perpetuate through an elitist educational system which emphasized the art of rhetoric. Given the great sin of the sophistic movement was its boasting . . . Paul made the Jeremiah prohibition against boasting about wisdom, status and achievement a primary text in this critique of the Corinthian sophistic movement." Bruce Winter, *Philo and Paul among the Sophists: Alexandrian and Corinthian Responses to a Julio-Claudian Movement*, 2nd ed. (Grand Rapids, MI: Eerdmans, 2002), 253–54. Duane Litfin makes a similar case, arguing that Paul is defining his role as a "herald" over and against the classical "orator" or rhetoric of Corinth: "Both his physical appearance and his speaking itself were deficient, even contemptible, by the sophisticated standards of Greek rhetoric (2 Cor. 10:10). Paul was simply out of his league. These people were accustomed to the *euglottia* ("beautiful speech") of orators of the caliber of Favorinus, that paragon of Greek culture whose eloquence was both *sophos* ("wise") and *potimos* ("sweet, pleasant"). [Philostratus, *Lives of the Sophists* (Cambridge, MA: Harvard University Press, 1998), 489, 491.] . . . Such a one as this could impress the Corinthians. But by this standard the apostle was an embarrassing figure. Whatever else one could say for him, he was woefully short by the stringent criteria of genuine Greek eloquence. He was simply a layman (*idiotes*, 2 Cor. 11:6) as a speaker. He appeared to lack the high-octane ability to discover convincing arguments and then sculpt them at will into irresistible phrases. He came far short of the polish and sophistication in word choice, in diction, in voice, in physical charm and self-possession that was indispensable to impress and move a Greco-Roman crowd." Duane Litfin, "Swallowing Our Pride: An Essay on the Foolishness of Preaching," in *Preach the Word: Essays on Expository Preaching: In Honor of R. Kent Hughes*, ed. Leland Ryken and Todd A. Wilson (Wheaton, IL: Crossway, 2007), 120.

"Not with Words of Eloquent Wisdom"

What then is he condemning? We know from 2 Corinthians 10:10 that Paul's opponents mocked him for lacking eloquence. They said, "His letters are weighty and strong, but his bodily presence is weak, and *his speech of no account.*" We also know from at least six sources that the sophists were present and influential in Corinth.[9] Unlike Paul, they put a huge premium on style and form as evidence of education and power and wisdom. They had probably influenced some in the church to admire their kind of eloquence and look for it in Christian teachers. Bruce Winter says, "Paul deliberately adopts an anti-sophistic stance and thus defends his church-planting activities in Corinth against a backdrop of sophistic conventions, perceptions, and categories."[10]

That's what we find in 1 Corinthians 1:17: "Christ did not send me to baptize but to preach the gospel, and *not with words of eloquent wisdom*, lest the cross of Christ be emptied of its power." So the way Paul is going to oppose the eloquence of the sophists is to show that it empties the cross. Why is that? Why does this view of eloquence empty the cross of power?

Verse 18 gives part of the reason: "For the word of the cross is folly to those who are perishing, but to us who are being saved it is the power of God." The reason the cross can't fit in with the eloquence of the sophists is that it is folly to them—that is, it is so destructive of human pride that those who aim at human praise through "rhetorically elaborated eloquence"[11] and "an elitist educational system"[12] could only see the cross as foolishness. The cross is the place our sin is seen as most horrible and where God's free grace shines most brightly. Both of these mean we deserve nothing. Therefore, the cross undercuts pride and exalts Christ, not us, and that made it foolish to the sophists.

We see this confirmed in verse 20: "Where is the one who is wise? Where is the scribe? Where is the debater of this age?"—the debater, the man who is so nimble with his tongue that he can take either side and win. He is smooth and clever and verbally agile. Truth and content

---

[9] Winter, *Philo and Paul*, 7–9, gives six sources for our knowledge of the sophist movement in Corinth. He concludes, "There can be no doubt . . . that sophists and their students were prominent in Corinth and played an important role in the life of the city." Ibid., 140.
[10] Ibid., 141.
[11] Ibid., 144n16.
[12] Ibid., 253.

are not the issue; rhetorical maneuvering is. Paul says at the end of verse 20, "Has not God made foolish the wisdom of the world?" The wisdom in view is not any deep worldview over against Christianity; it's the sophistry of using language to win debates and show oneself clever and eloquent and powerful.

So the eloquence Paul is rejecting is not so much any particular language conventions but the exploitation of language to exalt self and belittle or ignore the crucified Lord. Notice the contrast again in chapter 2, verses 1–2: "And I, when I came to you, brothers, did not come proclaiming to you the testimony of God with lofty speech or wisdom. For I decided to know nothing among you except Jesus Christ and him crucified." The point is: Wherever I meet scribes and debaters who bolster their ego with language jousting and leave the cross in the shadows, I am going to bring it out of the shadows and showcase it totally. I will refuse to play their language games.

The Marks of Good Eloquence

So if there is good eloquence (what I mean by poetic effort) and bad eloquence (what Paul is condemning in 1 Corinthians), we are now seeing two criteria of what is good. The good eloquence humbles itself and exalts Christ. This is most clearly seen in 1 Corinthians 1:26–31. Paul turns the tables on the sophists' love affair with boasting.[13]

> Consider your calling, brothers: not many of you were wise accord-
> ing to worldly standards, not many were powerful, not many were
> of noble birth. But God chose what is foolish in the world to shame
> the wise; God chose what is weak in the world to shame the strong;
> God chose what is low and despised in the world, even things that
> are not, to bring to nothing things that are, so that no human being
> might boast in the presence of God.

God's design, both in the cross and in election, is "that no human being might boast in the presence of God" (v. 29). That is the first criterion of good eloquence: *It does not come from pride or feed boasting. It does not come from an ego in search of exaltation through clever speech.*

---

[13] "The great sin of the sophistic movement was its boasting." Ibid.

Then he continues in verses 30–31,

> And because of him you are in Christ Jesus, who became to us wisdom from God, righteousness and sanctification and redemption, so that, as it is written, "Let the one who boasts, boast in the Lord."

The second design of God, not only in the cross and in election, but also in the sovereign grace of regeneration (v. 30, "*Because of him* you are in Christ Jesus") is that all boasting be boasting in the Lord Jesus—the one who was crucified and raised. "Let the one who boasts, boast in the Lord." So the second criterion of good eloquence is that it exalts Christ—*especially the crucified Christ.*

Self-Humbling, Christ-Exalting Poetic Effort

So here is the first reason why I don't think this book contradicts 1 Corinthians 1:17, where Paul says, "*Not with words of eloquent wisdom,*" or 1 Corinthians 2:1–2, where he says, "*[Not] with lofty speech or wisdom.*" The point of both these texts is not that all poetic effort (or call it Christ-exalting eloquence) is wrong. The point is that pride-sustaining, self-exalting use of words for a show of human wisdom is incompatible with finding your life and your glory in the cross of Christ. Rather, we should govern our use of words by these double criteria: self-humiliation and Christ-exaltation.

If we put these two criteria in front of all our poetic effort—all our attempts to make an impact through word selection and word arrangement and word delivery—we will be guarded from the kind of eloquence Paul rejected.

2. CHRIST-EXALTING CHRISTIAN ELOQUENCE MAY NOT BE THE REASON THE CROSS IS REJECTED

The second reason I don't think poetic effort is alien to Christ-exalting, self-humbling communication is this: accusations that eloquence is the problem are sometimes misdirected. This is not proof of the point. It is simply a removal of a misused counterargument.

Benjamin Franklin's Stumbling Block

In the spring of 1740, George Whitefield was in Philadelphia preaching outdoors to thousands of people. Benjamin Franklin attended most of these messages. Franklin, who did not believe what Whitefield was preaching, commented on these perfected sermons,

> His delivery . . . was so improved by frequent repetition, that every accent, every emphasis, every modulation of voice, was so perfectly well turned, and well placed, that *without being interested in the subject, one could not help being pleased with the discourse*: a pleasure of much the same kind with that received from an excellent piece of music.[14]

This is a fearful thing—to speak for Christ and be praised for our eloquence, not our Christ. But before we jump to the conclusion that Whitefield was neglecting Paul's counsel not to empty the cross by his eloquence, consider this. I believe there are people who have listened to my own preaching for years without grasping with their hearts what I was saying. They remained spiritually dead to what I was saying in spite of many changes in the manner of preaching—from the simplest to the most complex, from the tenderest to the toughest, from suspenseful story to careful argument. Yet they kept coming back, not because they loved what I said, but because they enjoyed the way I said it. They would tell me so. I have met with them one-on-one, pleaded with them, warned them, rebuked them, prayed over them. Yet, as far as I could tell, they remained blind to "the light of the gospel of the glory of Christ" (2 Corinthians 4:4). I detected no spiritual taste for the truth and beauty of Christ.

I do not believe this was because I had emptied the cross of its power through vain eloquence in all those messages. Rather, I believe it was owing to what Paul said in 2 Corinthians 2:15–16: "We are the aroma of Christ to God among those who are being saved and among those who are perishing, to one a fragrance from death to death, to the other a fragrance from life to life." In other words, the preacher's vanity and carnal eloquence are not the only stumbling blocks to faith.

---

[14] Harry Stout, *The Divine Dramatist* (Grand Rapids, MI: Eerdmans, 1991), 104 (emphasis added).

Jesus, John the Baptist, and the Stumbling Block of Truth

Herod would one day behead John the Baptist, but he could not stop listening to him: "When he heard him, he was greatly perplexed, and yet he heard him gladly" (Mark 6:20). Similarly with Jesus himself: "The great throng heard him gladly" (Mark 12:37), but very few understood what he was saying and truly believed. Jesus and John the Baptist were not tickling the ears of kings and people with clever speech or vain eloquence. They were not nullifying the words of Paul. Yet, their speech was "seasoned with salt" (Colossians 4:6) and caused kings and commoners to keep coming back.

Jesus said, "I told you, and you do not believe. The works that I do in my Father's name bear witness about me, but you do not believe because you are not among my sheep. My sheep hear my voice, and I know them, and they follow me" (John 10:25–27). Perhaps Jesus would have spoken this over Benjamin Franklin when he refused to believe in the message of George Whitefield. Perhaps Whitefield's eloquence was not an obstacle to his faith but an excuse of his unbelief, while others found it to be the pathway to the cross.

3. GOD INSPIRED MEN TO MAKE POETIC EFFORT

The third reason I don't think the apostle Paul (or any other biblical writer) ruled out poetic effort in the service of Christ is that God himself inspired men to make poetic effort in the writing of Scripture. We have already seen that in the very argument against vain human eloquence, Paul chose words that were highly out of the ordinary to strike an unforgettable blow: "The foolishness of God" and "The weakness of God" (1 Corinthians 1:25). This is the kind of thing I mean by poetic effort. This is a kind of shock-eloquence, and he used it while condemning vain eloquence.

Paul's Poetic Effort

This wasn't the only place Paul chose words that were unusual or metaphorical or emotionally impactful when he could have used words less surprising or moving or stabbing. For example,

- he called loveless speaking in tongues "a noisy gong or a clanging cymbal" (1 Corinthians 13:1);
- he described our incomplete knowledge on this earth compared with knowledge in heaven as the difference between a child's stammering and an adult's reasoning, and as seeing in a mirror dimly (1 Corinthians 13:11–12);
- he dared to compare the Lord's coming again to the coming of a thief (1 Thessalonians 5:2);
- he sought to waken the Thessalonians to his affections by saying, "We were gentle among you, like a nursing mother taking care of her own children" (1 Thessalonians 2:7);
- in 2 Corinthians 11 and 12, he dared to play on the enemy's field of boasting, beat them at their own game, then called himself a fool for doing it: "I am speaking as a fool—I also dare to boast of that" (2 Corinthians 11:21) and "I have been a fool!" (2 Corinthians 12:11);
- he calls his own weak body a jar "of clay" (2 Corinthians 4:7), and in another place a "tent" (2 Corinthians 5:2);
- he refers to himself and the apostles as "the filth of the world, and . . . the offscouring of all things" (1 Corinthians 4:13 KJV);
- he says that his highest moral attainments without Christ are "rubbish" (Philippians 3:8);
- he refers to fickle listeners as having "itching ears" (2 Timothy 4:3); and
- he describes our sins as written in a record and nailed with Jesus to the cross (Colossians 2:14).

This is what I mean by poetic effort. All these words are images laden with verbal power and evocative potential. He strove not to be boring. Not to be bland. He aimed to strike blows with feathers ("nursing mother") and stones ("fool," "rubbish," and "filth").

The Pervasive Poetic Effort of Scripture

Whole books have been written on the stunning richness and variety of language in the Bible. Addressing the question of how much of God's inspired Word is poetry, Leland Ryken asks and answers,

> Given the combined presence of parallelism and a heavy reliance on figurative language, how much of the Bible ranks as poetry?

One-third of the Bible is not too high an estimate. Whole books of the Bible are poetic: Job, Psalms, Proverbs, Song of Solomon. A majority of Old Testament prophecy is poetic in form. Jesus is one of the most famous poets of the world. Beyond these predominantly poetic parts of the Bible, figurative language appears throughout the Bible, and whenever it does, it requires the same type of analysis given to poetry.[15]

In Hosea 12:10, God himself says, "I have also spoken by the prophets, and I have multiplied visions, and used similitudes" (KJV). In other words, God himself claims to have put it in the minds of biblical writers to think of analogies and comparisons and metaphors and similes and symbols and parables—to search out words that point to reality in indirect ways, rather than always describing things directly with the least imaginative words.

The poet John Donne says, "The Holy Ghost in penning the Scriptures delights himself, not only with a propriety, but with a delicacy, and harmony, and melody of language; with height of Metaphors, and other figures, which may work greater impressions upon the Readers."[16] John Calvin cites Isaiah as an example: "Let us pay attention to the style of Isaiah which is not only pure and elegant, but also is ornamented with high art—from which we may learn that eloquence may be of great service to faith."[17]

Pascal and Paul on Pleasing the Hearer

The point is not that these verbal choices are decisive in bringing about the greatest goals of language. God alone decides that. The point is that, short of these highest goals, God seems to have ordained that typically some uses of language awaken, hold interest, and provoke to thought better than others so that the message might more clearly be seen and considered. Pascal writes,

---

[15] Leland Ryken, "'I Have Used Similitudes': The Poetry of the Bible," *Bibliotheca Sacra* 147 (July 1990), 259–60.

[16] John Donne, *The Sermons of John Donne*, ed. George R. Potter and Evelyn M. Simpson (Berkeley, CA: University of California Press, 1953–1962), 6:55.

[17] "Quoted in Calvin and the Bible," from *Selected Shorter Writings of Benjamin B. Warfield*, ed. John E. Meeter, vol. 1 (Presbyterian and Reformed Publishing Company, 1970). Originally from *The Presbyterian*, (June 30, 1909), 7–8.

> Eloquence is an art of saying things in such a way—(1) that those to whom we speak may listen to them without pain and with pleasure; (2) that they feel themselves interested, so that self-love leads them more willingly to reflection upon it.[18]

No doubt, there is eloquence that displeases the hearer, but Pascal's main point is that arresting and holding the listener (or reader) is a means to other ends. Surely the apostle Paul would have included his speech in the "everything" when he said, "I try to please everyone in everything I do, not seeking my own advantage, but that of many, that they may be saved" (1 Corinthians 10:33). It is not the pleasing that saves. God saves. But Paul believed acting (and speaking) a certain way could advance that salvation better than other ways. And he believed this, even though God can use any kind of speech he please as a means of salvation.

At the merely natural level, we are all dull and are served well when language claps its hands and wakes us up to pay attention. George Eliot in the novel *Middlemarch* speaks to this through one of her characters,

> We do not expect people to be deeply moved by what is not unusual. . . . If we had a keen vision and feeling of all ordinary human life, it would be like hearing the grass grow and the squirrel's heartbeat, and we should die of that roar which lies on the other side of silence. As it is, the quickest of us walk about well wadded with stupidity.[19]

Proverbs and Isaiah for Example

This may be one reason why the Bible is filled with every manner of literary device to add natural impact: acrostics, alliteration, analogies, anthropomorphism, assonance, cadence, chiasmus, consonance, dialogue, hyperbole, irony, metaphor, meter, onomatopoeia, paradox, parallelism, repetition, rhyme, satire, simile—they're all there, and more. Take a small sampling of these images from Proverbs and Isaiah only. They could be increased hundreds of times.

---

[18] Blaise Pascal, *Pensées* (New York: Dutton, 1958), Kindle Edition.
[19] George Eliot, *Middlemarch*, chap. 20 (1874), quoted in Donoghue, *On Eloquence*, 77.

- Bread gained by deceit is sweet to a man, but afterward his mouth will be full of gravel. (Proverbs 20:17)
- The lips of knowledge are a precious jewel. (Proverbs 20:15)
- A king's wrath is like the growling of a lion, but his favor is like dew on the grass. (Proverbs 19:12)
- Gracious words are like a honeycomb, sweetness to the soul and health to the body. (Proverbs 16:24)
- The name of the LORD is a strong tower; the righteous man runs into it and is safe. (Proverbs 18:10)
- Whoever trusts in his riches will fall, but the righteous will flourish like a green leaf. (Proverbs 11:28)
- A rich man's wealth is his strong city; the poverty of the poor is their ruin. (Proverbs 10:15)
- The tongue of the righteous is choice silver; the heart of the wicked is of little worth. (Proverbs 10:20)
- Like vinegar to the teeth and smoke to the eyes, so is the sluggard to those who send him. (Proverbs 10:26)
- Can a man carry fire next to his chest and his clothes not be burned? Or can one walk on hot coals and his feet not be scorched? So is he who goes in to his neighbor's wife; none who touches her will go unpunished. (Proverbs 6:27–29)
- Save yourself like a gazelle from the hand of the hunter, like a bird from the hand of the fowler. (Proverbs 6:5)
- Poverty will come upon you like a robber, and want like an armed man. (Proverbs 6:11)
- The lips of a forbidden woman drip honey, and her speech is smoother than oil. (Proverbs 5:3)
- [Wisdom] is a tree of life to those who lay hold of her; those who hold her fast are called blessed. (Proverbs 3:18)
- Wisdom cries aloud in the street, in the markets she raises her voice. (Proverbs 1:20)
- Wine is a mocker, strong drink a brawler, and whoever is led astray by it is not wise. (Proverbs 20:1).
- The terror of a king is like the growling of a lion; whoever provokes him to anger forfeits his life. (Proverbs 20:2)
- The spirit of man is the lamp of the LORD, searching all his innermost parts. (Proverbs 20:27)
- The heart of Ahaz and the heart of his people shook as the trees of the forest shake before the wind. (Isaiah 7:2)

- Do not let your heart be faint because of these two smoldering stumps of firebrands, at the fierce anger of Rezin and Syria and the son of Remaliah. (Isaiah 7:4)
- In that day the Lord will whistle for the fly [Pharaoh] that is at the end of the streams of Egypt, and for the bee [Sennacherib] that is in the land of Assyria. (Isaiah 7:18)
- They rejoice before you as with joy at the harvest, as they are glad when they divide the spoil. (Isaiah 9:3)
- Shall the axe boast over him who hews with it, or the saw magnify itself against him who wields it? As if a rod should wield him who lifts it, or as if a staff should lift him who is not wood! (Isaiah 10:15)
- The remnant of the trees of his forest will be so few that a child can write them down. (Isaiah 10:19)
- Behold, the Lord God of hosts will lop the boughs with terrifying power; the great in height will be hewn down, and the lofty will be brought low. (Isaiah 10:33)
- There shall come forth a shoot from the stump of Jesse, and a branch from his roots shall bear fruit. (Isaiah 11:1)
- They shall not hurt or destroy in all my holy mountain; for the earth shall be full of the knowledge of the Lord as the waters cover the sea. (Isaiah 11:9)
- They will be in anguish like a woman in labor. . . . Their faces will be aflame. (Isaiah 13:8)
- And like a hunted gazelle, or like sheep with none to gather them, each will turn to his own people, and each will flee to his own land. (Isaiah 13:14)
- Like fleeing birds, like a scattered nest, so are the daughters of Moab at the fords of the Arnon. (Isaiah 16:2)
- Behold, the Lord . . . will seize firm hold on you and whirl you around and around, and throw you like a ball into a wide land. (Isaiah 22:17–18)
- And I will fasten him like a peg in a secure place, and he will become a throne of honor to his father's house. And they will hang on him the whole honor of his father's house. (Isaiah 22:23–24)
- Moab shall be trampled down in his place, as straw is trampled down in a dunghill. And he will spread out his hands in the midst of it as a swimmer spreads his hands out to swim, but the Lord will lay low his pompous pride. (Isaiah 25:10–11)

- Like a pregnant woman who writhes and cries out in her pangs when she is near to giving birth, so were we because of you, O LORD; we were pregnant, we writhed, but we have given birth to wind. (Isaiah 26:17–18)
- As when a hungry man dreams, and behold, he is eating and awakes with his hunger not satisfied, or as when a thirsty man dreams, and behold, he is drinking and awakes faint, with his thirst not quenched, so shall the multitude of all the nations be that fight against Mount Zion. (Isaiah 29:8)
- This iniquity shall be to you like a breach in a high wall, bulging out, and about to collapse, whose breaking comes suddenly, in an instant. (Isaiah 30:13)
- A thousand shall flee at the threat of one; at the threat of five you shall flee, till you are left like a flagstaff on the top of a mountain, like a signal on a hill. (Isaiah 30:17)

The Invitation to Join Scripture in Its Poetic Effort

If the poetic effort of the wise man in Proverbs and the prophet Isaiah are not undermining to the spiritual purpose of Scripture to humble pride, point to Christ, waken hope, and lead to faith, then we will not be surprised that it seems God invites us to join him in this creativity of impactful and striking imagery in language. He beckons us with words like these:

> To make an apt answer is a joy to a man, and a word in season, how good it is! (Proverbs 15:23)

> The wise of heart is called discerning, and sweetness of speech increases persuasiveness. (Proverbs 16:21)

> A word fitly spoken is like apples of gold in a setting of silver. (Proverbs 25:11)

> Like a lame man's legs, which hang useless, is a proverb in the mouth of fools. (Proverbs 26:7)

> Let your speech always be gracious, seasoned with salt. (Colossians 4:6)

Whatever you do, in *word* or deed, do everything in the name of the Lord Jesus, giving thanks to God the Father through him. (Colossians 3:17)

In other words, give thought to the aptness and seasonableness and fitness and timing and appropriateness of your words. And make all of them an honor to the name of the Lord Jesus.

4. MANY WHO HAVE MADE POETIC EFFORT HAVE BEEN HUMBLE, OTHERS-ORIENTED PEOPLE

I know that many have been vain and self-exalting in their use of eloquence. If that were not true, Paul would not have written 1 Corinthians 1–4, and I would not be writing this introduction the way I am. Not only have there been such people, but we ourselves are prone to be that way. Pride lurks in every human heart. Christ died for this sin so that we might die to it and live in humble righteousness (1 Peter 2:24). But while we live in this fallen world, we must reckon it to be dead again and again. We must, so to speak, put it to death daily (Luke 9:23; 1 Corinthians 15:31; Colossians 3:5).

George Herbert: Less Than the Least of God's Mercies

Nevertheless, there have been truly humble persons who have aimed their poetic effort at the benefit of others and not at their self-exaltation. George Herbert, as we will see shortly, was a country pastor whose unpublished poems he offered on his deathbed to his trusted friend Nicholas Ferrar with these words to the courier:

> Sir, I pray deliver this little book to my dear brother Ferrar, and tell him he shall find in it a picture of the many spiritual conflicts that have passed betwixt God and my soul, before I could subject mine to the will of Jesus my Master, in whose service I have now found perfect freedom; desire him to read it: and then, if he can think it may turn to the advantage of any dejected poor soul, let it be made public; if not, let him burn it; for I and it are less than the least of God's mercies.[20]

---

[20] Quotation from Izaak Walton, *The Life of Mr. George Herbert* (1670), quoted in John Tobin, ed., *George Herbert: The Complete English Poems* (New York: Penguin Books, 1991), 310–11.

Here is the combination of humility ("Less than the least of God's mercies") and love for others ("If he can think it may turn to the advantage of any dejected poor soul"). Yet I doubt that there ever has been a more accomplished craftsman of poetic language than George Herbert.

Whitefield Humbled by the Doctrine of Election

George Whitefield, the eighteenth-century British evangelist, was the sensation of his day, on both sides of the Atlantic. Yet God led him to biblical views of sin and salvation that cut him down to size. He said,

> For my part I cannot see how true humbleness of mind can be attained without a knowledge of [the doctrine of election]; and though I will not say, that every one who denies election is a bad man, yet I will say, with that sweet singer, Mr. Trail, it is a very bad sign: such a one, whoever he be, I think cannot truly know himself; for, if we deny election, we must, partly at least, glory in ourselves; but our redemption is so ordered, that no flesh should glory in the Divine presence; and hence it is, that the pride of man opposes this doctrine, because, according to this doctrine, and no other, "he that glories must glory only in the Lord."[21]

The testimony of others, especially the lowly, is that he was a man of love. They did not smell the stench of pride or manipulation or abuse in his eloquence. They felt loved. For example, Phillis Wheatley, a black servant girl at age seventeen, wrote a poetic tribute to Whitefield titled,

AN ELEGIAC POEM ON THE DEATH OF THAT CELEBRATED DIVINE, AND EMINENT SERVANT OF JESUS CHRIST, THE LATE REVEREND, AND PIOUS GEORGE WHITEFIELD

It contained these lines:

> When his AMERICANS were burden'd sore,
> When streets were crimson'd with their guiltless gore!
> Unrival'd friendship in his breast now strove:
> The fruit thereof was charity and love.[22]

---

[21] Michael A. G. Haykin, ed., *The Revived Puritan: The Spirituality of George Whitefield* (Dundas, Ontario: Joshua, 2000), 97–98.
[22] Phillis Wheatley, "An Elegiac Poem on the Death of That Celebrated Divine, and Eminent Servant of Jesus Christ, the Late Reverend, and Pious George Whitefield," (1771), in *A Celebration of Women Writers,*

She was referring to American blacks. So, at least in her case, the eloquence of the man became not the exaltation of self but the expression of love.

C. S. Lewis's "Magisterial Humility"

C. S. Lewis was perhaps the most popular apologist for Christianity in the twentieth century. He is certainly the most widely read apologist today from the twentieth century. But Lewis, too, had come to Christ as the center of his world and the Savior of mind and soul and verbal skill. Owen Barfield, who knew him well, describes him as having a "magisterial humility."[23] I take this to mean that he carried his magisterial knowledge and ability lightly.

Lewis gives an unwitting description of himself when he says that the early Protestants had a "buoyant humility." "From this buoyant humility, this farewell to the self with all its good resolutions, anxiety, scruples, and motive-scratchings, all the Protestant doctrines originally sprang. . . . Relief and buoyancy are the characteristic notes."[24] Walter Hooper, his secretary, says,

> Although Lewis owned a huge library, he possessed few of his own works. His phenomenal memory recorded almost everything he had read except his own writings—an appealing fault. Often, when I quoted lines from his own poems he would ask who the author was. He was very great scholar, but no expert in the field of C. S. Lewis.[25]

One gets the impression that his "omnivorous attentiveness"[26] to the world and the people outside him had freed him in a wonderfully healthy way from the kind of self-preoccupation that angles for attention or praise. His poetic effort—whether in fiction or nonfiction—was strewn with imaginative ways of seeing and saying things, but it all seemed to serve others. One of the most striking things he ever said for an Oxford professor of literature was this:

Mary Mark Ockerbloom, ed., accessed January 13, 2014, http://www.digital.library.upenn.edu/women/wheatley/whitefield/whitefield.html.

[23] C. S. Lewis, *Poems*, ed. Walter Hooper (New York: Harcourt, Brace & World, 1964), vi.

[24] C. S. Lewis, *Poetry and Prose in the Sixteenth Century: The Oxford History of English Literature* (Oxford: Clarendon Press, 1954), 33–34.

[25] Lewis, *Poems*, vii.

[26] Alan Jacobs, *The Narnian* (New York: Harper One, 2005), xxi.

The Christian knows from the outset that the salvation of a single soul is more important than the production or preservation of all the epics and tragedies in the world: and as for superiority, he knows that the vulgar since they include most of the poor probably include most of his superiors.[27]

Poetic Effort That Does Not Empty the Cross

The human heart is deceitful above all things and desperately corrupt. We are capable of taking the most humbling theology and the most humbling experiences and turn them into props for pride. I am sure Herbert, Whitefield, and Lewis fell prey to that temptation. But I don't believe it was their deepest identity. Their egos had been humbled by the gospel of Jesus Christ, and their hearts had been turned outward toward the world. When they made poetic effort, they did it not to exalt themselves and empty the cross but to see and savor and show the truth and beauty of God—that is, they did it out of love.

5. SAYING NEWLY IS A WAY OF SEEING AND SAVORING NEWLY

A fifth reason I don't think Paul meant to condemn all poetic effort is that from my own experience poetic effort is not only helpful for others in *speaking* the glories of Christ but also helpful for me in *seeing* them and *savoring* them. This is the real origin of this book. George Herbert was the main inspiration.

Poetic Effort as Fellowship with Christ

In his poem called "Quidditie," Herbert has these lines about what writing poetry is for him:

> It is no office, art, or news;
> Nor the Exchange, or busie Hall;
> But it is that which while I use
> I am with thee. . . .[28]

---

[27] C. S. Lewis, "Christianity and Literature" in *Christian Reflections* (Grand Rapids, MI: Eerdmans, 1967), 10.
[28] George Herbert, "The Quidditie," in Helen Wilcox, ed., *The English Poems of George Herbert* (Cambridge: Cambridge University Press, 2007), 254.

His poems are "that which while I use I am with Thee." This put into words what I have found to be true for decades. The effort to put the truth of God, and all his ways and works, into fresh language—something that may have never been spoken before—is a way of coming near to God, because of seeing and feeling more suitably. "While I use [that is while I make poetic effort], I am with Thee."

Herbert confirmed for me in his experience what has been an indispensable part of my preaching and writing. I don't mean just the writing of poems but also the writing of sermons and books and letters and most anything else that matters. Every sermon was an opportunity not just to *say* but to *see* and *savor*. Every effort to speak the wonders of the Word of God became a fresh seeing and a fresh savoring. The pressure to prepare a fresh word from God week by week was one of the greatest gifts of my life. The effort to say beautifully was a way of seeing beauty. The effort to put a glimpse of glory into striking or moving words made the glimpse grow. The effort to find worthy words for Christ opened to me more fully the worth of Christ.

I think this is true for everyone. And that is one of the reasons I have written this book.

6. Three Great Examples: George Herbert, George Whitefield, and C. S. Lewis

Finally, I believe that self-humbling, Christ-exalting eloquence—or poetic effort, as I am calling it in this book—is valid and important for Christian living and speaking because the three subjects of this book bear it out in their lives. I commend them to you for your own inspiration and guidance. All three of them, of course, are vastly more gifted than I am and perhaps than you are. Don't let that put you off. I come nowhere close to the poetic gifting of George Herbert, the dramatic power of George Whitefield, or the imaginative power of C. S. Lewis. But, O, what they have shown me of truth and beauty and how to see them and say them. The glory of Christ is brighter and clearer and sweeter for me because of their poetic effort—the effort to see and savor and speak the glories they have seen in fresh and powerful ways. I thank God them.

Yes, there is humble, Christ-exalting eloquence. Yes, poetic effort is good. It is not the decisive factor in salvation. God is. But faith and all its fruits come by hearing, and hearing by the Word (Romans 10:17; Galatians 3:5). That Word in the Bible is pervasively eloquent—words are put together in a way to give great impact. And God invites us to create our own fresh phrases for his glory, not ours. And in the mystery of his sovereign grace, he will glorify himself in us and in the hearts of others in spite of and because of the words we have chosen. In that way, he will keep us humble and get all the glory for himself.

The Quidditie

My God, a verse is not a crown,
No point of honour, or gay suit,
No hawk, or banquet, or renown,
Nor a good sword, nor yet a lute:

It cannot vault, or dance, or play;
It never was in *France* or *Spain*;
Nor can it entertain the day
With a great stable or demain:

It is no office, art, or news;
Nor the Exchange, or busie Hall;
But it is that which while I use
I am with thee: and *Most take all*.

George Herbert

1

"WHILE I USE I AM WITH THEE"

The Life and Poetry of George Herbert

If you go to the mainstream poetry website *Poetry Foundation* and click on George Herbert, what you read is this: "He is . . . enormously popular, deeply and broadly influential, and arguably the most skillful and important British devotional lyricist of this or any other time."[1] This is an extraordinary tribute to a man who never published a single poem in English during his lifetime and died as an obscure country pastor when he was thirty-nine. But there are reasons for his enduring influence. And some of those reasons are why I have written this book.

HIS SHORT LIFE

George Herbert was born April 3, 1593, in Montgomeryshire, Wales. He died a month before his fortieth birthday on March 1, 1633. He was the seventh of ten children born to Richard and Magdalene Herbert, but his father died when he was three, leaving ten children, the oldest of which was thirteen. This didn't put them in financial hardship, however, because Richard's estate, which he left to Magdalene, was sizeable.

---

[1] "George Herbert," *Poetry Foundation*, accessed December 9, 2013, http://www.poetryfoundation.org/bio /george-herbert.

It was twelve years before Magdalene married again, this time to Sir John Danvers who was twenty years younger than she was and just two years older than her eldest son. But he was a good father to the family during the eighteen years of marriage until Magdalene's death in 1627. George Herbert kept in touch with his stepfather and eventually made him the executor of his will. Herbert never knew him as a father in the home because the year John and Magdalene married was the year Herbert began his studies at Trinity College Cambridge.

Herbert had been an outstanding student at a Westminster preparatory school, writing Latin essays when he was eleven years old, which would later be published. And now at Cambridge, he distinguished himself in the study of classics. He graduated second in a class of 193 in 1612 with a bachelor of arts, and then in 1616, he took his master of arts and became a major fellow of the university.

In 1619, he was elected public orator of Cambridge University. This was a prestigious post with huge public responsibility. Herbert wrote to his stepfather what it meant to be elected the orator.

> The finest place in the University, though not the gainfullest. . . .
> For the Orator writes all the University letters, makes all the orations, be it to King, Prince, or whatever comes to the University, to requite these pains, he takes place next to the Doctors, is at all their assemblies and meetings, and sits above the Proctors. . . . And such like Gaynesses. Which will please a young man well.[2]

This is going to be one of the most important insights into his life because the academic stimulation, the prominence even in the king's court,[3] and the pleasures of it all would prove the great battleground over his call to the pastoral ministry.

Eleven years after his election to the oratorship, on the day of his induction to the parish ministry at Bemerton, he would say,

> I can now behold the Court with an impartial eye, and see plainly that it is made up of fraud, titles and flattery, and many other such

---

[2] Quoted in Margaret Bottrall, *George Herbert* (London: John Murray, 1954), 13.
[3] "The Court was not merely a spring-board for men ambitious of public office; it was the focus of all talent, literary and artistic, and its patronage extended to preachers and divines as well as to the playwrights and poets." Ibid., 16.

empty, imaginary and painted pleasures: pleasures that are so empty as not to satisfy when they are enjoyed.[4]

But for now, there seemed good reasons to give himself to public service for the sake of the university and its relation to the wider civic life of the country. On top of the oratorship, he added a one-year term in Parliament in 1623–1624.

But the conflict of his soul over a call to the pastoral ministry intensified that year. And a vow he had made to his mother during his first year at Cambridge took hold in his heart. He submitted himself totally to God and to the ministry of a parish priest. He was ordained as a deacon in the Church of England in 1626 and then became the ordained priest of the little country church at Bemerton in 1630. There were never more than a hundred people in his church. The last three years of his life, he was a parson to a remote country parish.

At the age of thirty-six and in failing health, Herbert married Jane Danvers the year before coming to Bemerton, March 5, 1629. As the name suggests, she was a kinswoman of his stepfather. We only know about Herbert's marriage because of Izaak Walton's *Life of Mr George Herbert*, published in 1670. He says it was a happy four years. He and Jane never had children, though they adopted three nieces who had lost their parents. After fewer than three years in the ministry, Herbert died of tuberculosis, which he had suffered from most of his adult life. He was thirty-nine years old. His body lies under the chancel of the church, and there is only a simple plaque on the wall with the initials GH.

His Dying Gift

That's the bare outline of Herbert's life. And if that were all there was, nobody today would have ever heard of George Herbert. Even the fact that he wrote a short book known as *The Country Parson* would probably not have secured his place in memory. The reason anyone knows of George Herbert today, and the reason he is included in this volume, is because of something climactic that happened a few weeks before he died.

---

[4] Quoted in Pat Magee, *George Herbert: Rector of Bemerton* (Moxham Printers, 1977), 15.

His close friend Nicholas Ferrar sent a fellow pastor, Edmund Duncon, to see how Herbert was doing. On Duncon's second visit, Herbert knew that the end was near. So he reached for his most cherished earthly possession and said to Duncon,

> Sir, I pray deliver this little book to my dear brother Ferrar, and tell him he shall find in it a picture of the many spiritual conflicts that have passed betwixt God and my soul, before I could subject mine to the will of Jesus my Master, in whose service I have now found perfect freedom; desire him to read it: and then, if he can think it may turn to the advantage of any dejected poor soul, let it be made public; if not, let him burn it; for I and it are less than the least of God's mercies.[5]

That little book was a collection of 167 poems. Herbert's friend Nicholas Ferrar published it later that year, 1633, under the title *The Temple*. It went through four editions in three years, was steadily reprinted for a hundred years, and is still in print today. It established Herbert as one of the greatest religious poets of all time, though not one of these poems was published during his lifetime.

CENTURIES OF ACCOLADES

Forty-eight years after Herbert's death, Richard Baxter said, "Herbert speaks to God like one that really believeth a God, and whose business in this world is most with God. Heart-work and heaven-work make up his books."[6] William Cowper cherished Herbert's poetry in his struggle with depression.[7] Samuel Taylor Coleridge, nineteenth-century poet and critic, wrote to a member of the Royal Academy, "I find more substantial comfort now in pious George Herbert's *Temple* [the collection of his poems] . . . than in all the poetry since the poetry of Milton."[8]

Herbert's poetry is found in virtually every anthology of English

---

[5] Quotation from Izaak Walton, *The Life of Mr. George Herbert* (1670), quoted in John Tobin, ed., *George Herbert: The Complete English Poems* (New York: Penguin, 1991), 310–11.
[6] Quoted in Helen Wilcox, ed., *The English Poems of George Herbert* (Cambridge, UK: Cambridge University Press, 2007), xxi.
[7] Jane Falloon, *Heart in Pilgrimage: A Study of George Herbert* (Bloomington, IN: Author-House, 2007), ix.
[8] Quoted in Bottrall, *George Herbert*, 145.

literature. He is one of the very few great poets who is loved both by specialists and nonspecialists. He is loved for his technical rigor and his spiritual depth. T. S. Eliot said, "The exquisite variations of form in the . . . poems of *The Temple* show a resourcefulness of invention which seems inexhaustible, and for which I know no parallel in English poetry.[9] Margaret Bottrall agrees that Herbert "was an exquisite craftsman."[10] He was part of an era that prized meticulous care with language and poetry. Peter Porter writes that the fact "that Herbert is perhaps the most honest poet who ever wrote in English does not prevent his being also one of the most accomplished technicians of verse in the whole [Western] canon."[11]

REFORMED, POETIC MINISTRY FOR AN OPIUM ADDICT

We will come back to his craftsmanship shortly. But linger with me over the power of his poetry to minister deeply to the likes of an opium addict such as Samuel Coleridge. One of the reasons for this is the solid rock of God's sovereignty that Coleridge felt under Herbert's poems. This is a dimension of Herbert's poetry that, I would guess, few English literature classes address. But it is essential for understanding his poems. Gene Edward Veith wrote his doctoral dissertation on Herbert as a representative of *reformation spirituality*. He comments, to the surprise of many,

> Serious studies of George Herbert invariably come upon his Calvinism. Rather than its being seen as a solution, though, it has been treated as something of a problem. How is it that a theology associated with determinism, austerity, the impoverishment of the liturgy, and "Puritanism," with all of its negative connotations, can produce such winsome religious verse?[12]

---

[9] T. S. Eliot, *George Herbert* (Plymouth, UK: Northcote House, 1962), 36. In the introduction to this same volume, Peter Porter writes, "We begin by admiring the abruptness, go on to wonder at the singularity of the argument, sometimes even its bizarreness, but end up being awed by the moral rightness of what is said. We see why invention matters, why cleverness is not the enemy of seriousness. What else could have kept Herbert's poetry so fresh? Matthew Arnold's 'melancholy long withdrawing roar' of the sea of faith is no match for the ageless freshness of Herbert's epiphanic sound."
[10] Bottrall, *George Herbert*, 1.
[11] Peter Porter, "Introduction" in T. S. Eliot, *George Herbert*, 2.
[12] Gene Edward Veith, *Reformation Spirituality: The Religion of George Herbert* (Cranbury, NJ: Associated University Presses, 1985), 23.

Not What We Often Think about the Earliest Protestants

In partial answer to this question, Veith points out,

> Calvinism, attacked now for its strictness, was originally attacked for its permissiveness. Far from being ascetic, Calvinism was in conscious reaction to monastic asceticism, which rejected marriage and sexuality and insisted upon fasts and mortification of the flesh. Far from being a "theology of fear," Calvinism offered to believers, who had been taught to continually be terrified of hell, the assurance that salvation is free and that it can never be lost.[13]

Unless we put ourselves back into that period of history, we will likely bring some wrong assumptions to the task of grasping Herbert's Calvinism. C. S. Lewis wrote what remains one of the most authoritative histories of sixteenth-century literature, overflowing into the early 1600s. In it he makes this same point as he tries to free modern readers from misconceptions about the earliest Calvinists. Lewis observes that Charles Dickens's nineteenth-century character, "Mrs. Clennam, trying to expiate her early sin by a long life of voluntary gloom, was doing exactly what the first Protestants [of the sixteenth century] would have forbidden her to do."[14] Their experience was radically different:

> It springs directly out of a highly specialized religious experience. . . . The experience is that of catastrophic conversion. The man who has passed through it feels like one who has waked from nightmare into ecstasy. Like an accepted lover, he feels that he has done nothing, and never could have done anything, to deserve such astonishing happiness. . . . His own puny and ridiculous efforts would be as helpless to retain the joy as they would have been to achieve it in the first place. . . . From this buoyant humility, this farewell to the self with all its good resolutions, anxiety, scruples, and motive-scratchings, all the Protestant doctrines originally sprang. . . . Relief and buoyancy are the characteristic notes.[15]

---

[13] Ibid., 28.
[14] C. S. Lewis, *Poetry and Prose in the Sixteenth Century: The Oxford History of English Literature* (Oxford: Clarendon, 1954), 33.
[15] Ibid., 33–34.

RETHINKING "PURITAN"

The implication of this, Lewis says, is that "every association which now clings to the word *Puritan* has to be eliminated when we are thinking of the early Protestants. Whatever they were, they were not sour, gloomy, or severe; nor did their enemies bring any such charge against them."[16] For the Roman Catholic—Thomas More, for example—the Puritans were "dronke of the new must of lewd lightnes of mind and vayne gladnesse of harte."[17] "Protestantism," Lewis concludes, "was not too grim, but too glad, to be true."[18]

The Reformation doctrine of God's absolute sovereignty over the world, Lewis says, was "unemphasized because it was unquestioned, that every event, every natural fact, and every institution, is rooted in the supernatural. Every change of winds at sea, every change of dynasty at home, all prosperity and all adversity, is unhesitatingly referred to God. The writers do not argue about it, they know."[19]

Lewis ventures a comparison to help us break out of our misconceptions of the early Calvinists. He admits the analogy is risky: "It may be useful to compare the influence of Calvin on that age with the influence of Marx on our own; or even Marx and Lenin in one, for Calvin had both expounded the new system in theory and set it going in practice."[20] The point he's making is not about communism but about the youth and revolutionary impulse of the Calvinists:

> This will at least serve to eliminate the absurd idea that Elizabethan Calvinists were somehow grotesque, elderly people, standing outside the main forward current of life. In their own day they were, of course, the very latest thing. Unless we can imagine the freshness, the audacity, and (soon) the fashionableness of Calvinism, we shall get our whole picture wrong. . . . The fierce young don, the learned lady, the courtier with intellectual leanings, were likely to be Calvinists.[21]

So when Gene Veith writes an entire book on George Herbert's Calvinism, we must be careful not to import our own misconceptions. He

---

[16] Ibid., 34.
[17] Ibid., (original spelling of More's *Dialogue*, 3.2).
[18] Ibid.
[19] Ibid., 38.
[20] Ibid., 42.
[21] Ibid., 43.

was not a Puritan in his own time. He was a high-church Episcopalian. "During Herbert's lifetime, however, Calvinism was the norm, both for Episcopalian factions and for Presbyterian ones."[22] "The Anglican Church of Herbert's day, in its mainstream, was both ceremonial in its liturgy and Calvinist in its theology."[23]

What Made the Difference from John Donne

But not all clergy in the Church of England embraced Herbert's Calvinistic reformation spirituality. It is illuminating to note that John Donne, the close friend of Herbert's mother, did not share Herbert's Calvinism. Though his style influenced Herbert significantly, there is a marked difference in their devotional poetry. Here's the way Gene Veith puts it:

> It has been observed that Herbert never worries about hell, in marked contrast to John Donne's obsessive fear of damnation. This is perhaps the clearest evidence of Herbert's Calvinism, the point where dogma touches religious experience. For a Calvinist, hell is not a possibility for a Christian. Herbert believed in the perseverance of the saints, a doctrine that is perhaps the litmus test of a truly Calvinist spirituality.[24]

Therefore, as Veith shows, "The dynamics of Calvinism are also the dynamics of Herbert's poetry."[25] The heart of these "dynamics" is the sovereign intervention of God's grace into the rebellious human heart to subdue the mutiny against heaven and give a new allegiance to the true king of the world, Jesus Christ. Herbert experienced this, wrote about this, preached this, and prayed this.

> Thou hast exalted thy mercy above all things, and hast made our salvation, not our punishment, thy glory: so that then where sin abounded, not death but grace superabounded—accordingly, when we had sinned beyond any help in heaven or earth, then thou saidest, Lo, I come![26]

---

22 Ibid., 27.
23 Ibid., 30.
24 Veith, *Reformation Spirituality*, 34.
25 Ibid.
26 George Herbert, "The Author's Prayer before Sermon," in *A Priest to the Temple; Or, The Country Parson: His Character, and Rule of Life*, in Tobin, *George Herbert*, 261.

When there was no help from anywhere—when the case of the human heart is hopeless in its rebellion—God breaks in and saves. That is the heart of his Calvinism. Veith says Herbert's poem "The Collar" is "the supreme Calvinist poem,"

> dramatizing the depraved human will that insists on serving itself rather than God, in a state of intrinsic rebellion and growing chaos until God intervenes intruding upon the human will in a way that cannot be resisted, calling the sinner, effecting a response, and restoring order.[27]

THE COLLAR

I struck the board, and cry'd, No more.
           I will abroad.
What? shall I ever sigh and pine?
My lines and life are free; free as the rode,
     Loose as the winde, as large as store.
           Shall I be still in suit?
Have I no harvest but a thorn
To let me bloud, and not restore
What I have lost with cordiall fruit?
                     Sure there was wine
          Before my sighs did drie it: there was corn
          Before my tears did drown it.
     Is the yeare onely lost to me?
                Have I no bayes to crown it?
No flowers, no garlands gay? all blasted?
                All wasted?
Not so, my heart: but there is fruit,
                And thou hast hands.
     Recover all thy sigh-blown age
On double pleasures: leave thy cold dispute
Of what is fit, and not forsake thy cage,
                Thy rope of sands,
Which pettie thoughts have made, and made to thee
     Good cable, to enforce and draw,

---

[27] Veith, *Reformation Spirituality*, 34.

And be thy law,
While thou didst wink and wouldst not see.
Away; take heed:
I will abroad.
Call in thy deaths head there: tie up thy fears.
He that forbears
To suit and serve his need,
Deserves his load.
But as I rav'd and grew more fierce and wilde
At every word,
Me thoughts I heard one calling, *Childe*:
And I reply'd, *My Lord*.[28]

The Best News Coleridge Ever Heard

In other words, just as Herbert had prayed, "When we had sinned beyond any help in heaven or earth, then thou saidest, Lo, I come!" This sovereign intervention into the rebellious human heart—like the opium-addicted heart of Samuel Coleridge—was the best of news, and Coleridge saw more clearly than most people in his day that the criticisms of Calvinism often obscured the comfort of the doctrine itself. Here's the way he put it:

> If ever a book was calculated to drive men to despair, it is Bishop Jeremy Taylor's *On Repentance*. It first opened my eyes to Arminianism, and that Calvinism is *practically* a far more soothing and consoling system. . . . Calvinism (Archbishop Leighton's for example) compared with Taylor's Arminianism, is the lamb in wolf's skin to the wolf in the lamb's skin: the one is cruel in the phrases, the other in the doctrine.[29]

Remember, as we noted earlier, Coleridge had said, "I find more substantial comfort now in pious George Herbert's *Temple*, which I used to read to amuse myself with his quaintness, in short, only to laugh at, than in all the poetry since the poetry of Milton." This is because, as Veith argues, Herbert was the "clearest and most consistent poetic

---

[28] "The Collar," in Wilcox, *English Poems of George Herbert*, 526.
[29] Veith, *Reformation Spirituality*, 117.

voice"[30] of the Calvinism which Coleridge found to be life giving. Veith comments on Coleridge's words,

> Herbert is a lamb clothed in the wolf-skin of Calvinism. . . . Calvinism [as Coleridge says] "is cruel in the phrases," with its dreadful language of depravity and reprobation; Arminianism has gentle phrases (free will, universal atonement), but is cruel "in the doctrine." Coleridge, perhaps faced with the incapacity of his own will, his inability, for instance, to simply choose to stop taking opium, saw the consolation in a theology that based salvation not on the contingency of human will and efforts, but on the omnipotent will and unceasing effort of God.[31]

GOD'S DAILY SOVEREIGN WORK TO "MAKE" US

Herbert knew the answer to Coleridge's need. It was the answer to his own struggles. And it was not free will. It was not even an initial act of sovereign, delivering grace. It was *daily*, lifelong sovereign sustaining grace. In his poem "Giddinesse," Herbert laments the fragmented, fickle nature of man's heart—his heart.

> Oh what a thing is man! how farre from power,
> From setled peace and rest!
> He is some twentie sev'rall men at least
> Each sev'rall houre.

What is the remedy? Not just one act of new creation at the beginning of our life in Christ, but rather God's *daily* sovereign work as Creator to *make* us, not just mend us.

> Lord, mend or rather make us: one creation
> Will not suffice our turn:
> Except thou make us dayly, we shall spurn
> Our own salvation.[32]

Herbert continually celebrates the grace of God not only in his initial salvation but in God's ongoing returns and rescues from spiritual

---

[30] Ibid., 35.
[31] Ibid., 131–32.
[32] "Giddinesse," in Wilcox, *English Poems of George Herbert*, 446.

and emotional death. "How fresh, O Lord, how sweet and clean are thy returns! . . . After so many deaths I live."[33] Again, in a poem titled "Nature," he celebrates God's great "art" of subduing human rebellion and taking us captive repeatedly:

> Full of rebellion, I would die,
> Or fight, or travail, or denie
> That thou hast ought to do with me.
>   O tame my heart;
>   It is thy highest art
> To captivate strong holds to thee.[34]

SWEET SECURITY THROUGH MANY CONFLICTS OF SOUL

Herbert called his poems the record of his conflict with God.[35] But through them all, there is the resounding note of solid confidence in God's covenant with his people. This is why Coleridge found such help. And thousands of others have as well. Perhaps the clearest poem about our security in God's provision, even of our faith and our daily confession, is "The Holdfast."

> I threatened to observe the strict decree
>   Of my deare God with all my power & might.
>   But I was told by one, it could not be;
> Yet I might trust in God to be my light.
>
> Then will I trust, said I, in him alone.
>   Nay, ev'n to trust in him, was also his:
>   We must confesse, that nothing is our own.
> Then I confess that he my succor is:
>
> But to have naught is ours, not to confesse
>   That we have nought. I stood amaz'd at this,
>   Much troubled, till I heard a friend expresse,
> That all things were more ours by being his.

---

[33] "The Flower," in ibid., 568.
[34] "Nature," in ibid. 155.
[35] Tobin, *George Herbert*, 310–11.

What Adam had, and forfeited for all,
Christ keepeth now, who cannot fail or fall.[36]

This is what Coleridge felt as a precious gift from Herbert's poems: Utter honesty about what Herbert called "the many spiritual Conflicts that have passed betwixt God and my soul"[37] and the God-given confidence that all our faith, all our perseverance, all our safety, lies in Christ. "Nay, ev'n to trust in him, was also his." The sovereign, keeping power of God's love proves to be a profound comfort.

> We all acknowledge both thy power and love
> To be exact; transcendent, and divine;
> Who dost so strongly and so sweetly move,
> While all things have their will, yet none but thine.[38]

This is the sovereign permeation of all our supposed autonomy that every enslaved sinner desperately needs. "While all things have their will, yet none but thine." For an addict like Coleridge, this was the comforting sheep in wolf's clothing. This was the secret of hope for the hopelessly enchained—everyone.

The Beauty of His Craftsmanship

So from the springs of his Anglican,[39] Reformed[40] spiritual heritage, Herbert has nurtured wounded and hungry souls for centuries. And he has done it as one of the most gifted craftsmen the world of poetry has ever known. Not only is he regarded by many as "the greatest devotional poet in English,"[41] his skill in the use of language has earned him the high praises in the twentieth century from T. S. Eliot,[42]

---

[36] "The Holdfast," in Wilcox, *English Poems of George Herbert*, 499.

[37] Tobin, *George Herbert*, 311.

[38] "Providence," Wilcox, *English Poems of George Herbert*, 417.

[39] Gerard Manley Hopkins found his love of Herbert "his strongest tie to the English Church." Margaret Bottrall, *George Herbert*, 95.

[40] "George Herbert, the loyal Anglican, was more 'Puritan' in literary temper, than Andrew Marvell, the civil servant of the Puritan government." Veith, *Reformation Spirituality*, 31.

[41] Wilcox, *English Poems of George Herbert*, xxi. See also Veith's estimate: "George Herbert, measured by any standard—his craftsmanship, his mastery of language, his poetic and religious subtlety, the profoundness of his spiritual experience—may well be the greatest of all religious poets." Veith, *Reformation Spirituality*, 20.

[42] "When we take Herbert's collected poems and read industriously through the volume we cannot help being astonished both at the considerable number of pieces which are as fine as those in any anthology, and at what we may consider the spiritual stamina of the work. Throughout there is brainwork, and a very high level of intensity; his poetry is definitely an *oeuvre*, to be studied entire, and our gradual

W. H. Auden,[43] Gerard Manley Hopkins, Elizabeth Bishop, and Seamus Heaney.[44]

Herbert loved crafting language in new and powerful ways. It was for him a way of seeing and savoring and showing the wonders of Christ. The central theme of his poetry was the redeeming love of Christ,[45] and he labored with all his literary might to see it clearly, feel it deeply, and show it strikingly. We don't have a single sermon that he ever preached. None has survived the vagaries of history. One can only imagine that they would have been rich with the beauties of Christ. What we have is his poetry. And here the beauty of the *subject* is wedded to the beauty of his *craft*. What we are going to see is not only that the beauty of the subject inspired the beauty of the poetry, but more surprisingly, the effort to find beautiful poetic form helped Herbert see more of the beauty of his subject. The craft of poetry opened more of Christ for Herbert—and for us.

Of the 167 poems in *The Temple*, 116 are written with meters that are not repeated. This is simply incredible when you think about it. He created new kinds of structures for seventy percent of his poems. Peter Porter expresses the amazement poets feel when they encounter Herbert: "The practicing poet examining a Herbert poem is like someone bending over a Rolls-Royce engine. How is it all done? Why can't I make something so elaborate and yet so simple? Why is a machine which performs so well also so beautiful?"[46]

BEAUTY AND BEAUTEOUS WORDS

Herbert could not conceive of such a thing as a formless poem. The modern concept of free verse would probably have been incomprehensible to him. The poet's duty was to perceive and communicate beauty—which for Herbert meant the beauty of God. In the process, he would construct out of the chaos of experience and the mass of language an object that would reflect the beauty of the subject.[47]

---

appreciation of the poetry gives us a new impression of the man." T. S. Eliot quoted in Jane Falloon, *Heart in Pilgrimage: A Study of George Herbert*, x–xi.

[43] Auden said that George Herbert was one of the few artists of genius that he would have liked to have known personally. Cited from the "Introduction" by Peter Porter in Eliot, *George Herbert*, 3.

[44] Wilcox, *English Poems of George Herbert*, xxi.

[45] "His most frequent and dearest theme is the redemptive love of Christ." Bottrall, *George Herbert*, 88.

[46] Porter, "Introduction," in Eliot, *George Herbert*, 4.

[47] Joseph H. Summers, *George Herbert: His Religion and Art* (Cambridge, MA: Harvard University Press, 1954), 93.

> True beautie dwells on high: ours is a flame
> But borrow'd thence to light us thither.
> Beautie and beauteous words should go together.[48]

Beauty originates in God. It lights our little candle of beauty here as a way to lead us to God. Therefore, "beautie and beauteous words should go together." They should go together as a witness to the origin of beauty in God and as a way of leading us home to God.

ALL CONSECRATED TO GOD'S GLORY

In other words, Herbert never aimed at art for art's sake—technique for technique's sake. When he was seventeen years old, he wrote two sonnets for his mother. He sent them to her with a vow. He seemed to know already that he would give much of his life to poetry. The letter accompanying the poems to his mother lamented "the vanity of those many love poems that are daily writ, and consecrated to Venus" and that "so few are writ that look towards God and heaven." Then came his vow: "That my poor abilities in poetry, shall be all and ever consecrated to God's glory."[49]

He kept that vow in a radical way. "Not a single lyric in *The Temple* is addressed to a human being or written in honor of one."[50] He writes all 167 poems of *The Temple* as a record of his life with God. Herbert was moved to write with consummate skill because his only subject was consummately glorious. "The subject of every single poem in *The Temple*," Helen Wilcox says, "is, in one way or another, God."[51]

> How should I praise thee, Lord! how should my rymes
> Gladly engrave thy love in steel,
> If what my soul doth feel sometimes,
> My soul might ever feel![52]

His aim was to feel the love of God and to engrave it in the steel of human language for others to see and feel. Poetry was entirely for God, because everything is entirely for God. He wrote "The Elixer" precisely

---

[48] "Forerunners," in Wilcox, *English Poems of George Herbert*, 612.
[49] Joan Bennett, *Five Metaphysical Poets* (Cambridge: Cambridge University Press, 1964), 51.
[50] Bottrall, *George Herbert*, 134.
[51] Wilcox, *English Poems of George Herbert*, xxi.
[52] "The Temper (I)" in ibid., 193.

to give an account of how doing all things for God's sake turns them into something supremely valuable—whether it be sweeping a room or writing poetry.

"FOR THY SAKE"

"An *elixir* (conventional modern spelling) is a preparation used by alchemists in the attempt to change base metals into gold."[53] In this poem, it is the same as the "tincture" that makes the "mean" and lowly "grow bright and clean." It is the "famous stone" that turns all to gold. And what is this elixir? This tincture? This stone? It is the heart's intention: "For thy sake" (stanza four). So the truth he is celebrating in this poem is that intentionally referring all things to God gives them great worth (gold!), whatever they are. This is what he vowed to his mother he would do with all his poems.

THE ELIXER

Teach me, my God and King,
In all things thee to see,
And what I do in any thing,
To do it as for thee:

Not rudely, as a beast,
To runne into an action;
But still to make thee prepossest,
And give it his perfection.

A man that looks on glasse,
On it may stay his eye;
Or if he pleaseth, through it passe,
And then the heav'n espie.

All may of thee partake:
Nothing can be so mean,
Which with his tincture (for thy sake)
Will not grow bright and clean.

---

[53] Wilcox, *English Poems of George Herbert*, 641.

> A servant with this clause
> Makes drudgerie divine:
> Who sweeps a room, as for thy laws,
> Makes that and th' action fine.
>
> This is the famous stone
> That turneth all to gold:
> For that which God doth touch and own
> Cannot for lesse be told.[54]

In every stanza the "elixir" that turns all of life and poetry to gold is expressed in different ways:

Stanza one: "What I do in any thing to, do it as for thee."

Stanza two: "To make [God] prepossest" (having preeminence and ownership).

Stanza three: Looking not just at, but through, all things to see heaven.

Stanza four: "For thy sake."

Stanza five: "With this clause [for thy sake]," we beautify drudgery.

Stanza six: God is the one who touches the ordinary and turns it into gold.

"Secretarie of Thy Praise"

Poetry is one of those simple tasks of God's servant that needs to be touched by the elixir, the tincture, the stone and turned into God's praise. Herbert believed that since God ruled all things by his sacred providence, everything revealed God. Everything spoke of God. The role of the poet is to be God's echo. Or God's secretary. To me, Herbert's is one of the best descriptions of the Christian poet: "Secretarie of thy praise."

> O Sacred Providence, who from end to end
> Strongly and sweetly movest! shall I write,
> And not of thee, through whom my fingers bend
> To hold my quill? shall they not do thee right?

---

[54] "The Elixer," in ibid., 640–41.

Of all the creatures both in sea and land
Only to Man thou hast made known thy wayes,
And put the penne alone into his hand,
And made him Secretarie of thy praise.[55]

God bends Herbert's fingers around his quill. "Shall they not do thee right?" Shall I not be faithful secretary of thy praise—faithfully rendering—beautifully rendering—the riches of your truth and beauty? This is a high calling. And this is why so many of his poems are laments about his dullness and his impending loss of powers. He mourns the diminishing ability to "do thee right"—to be God's faithful secretary, to "praise thee brim-full."

Why do I languish thus, drooping and dull,
As if I were all earth?
O give me quicknesse, that I may with mirth
Praise thee brim-full![56]

LIVING AND WRITING TO SHOW GOD'S POWER

Herbert would die of tuberculosis at the age of thirty-nine. He was weakened by this disease most of his adult life—enduring "so many deaths." Therefore, his powers to write poetry came and went. This was a great sorrow. He lived to preach and write about the greatness of God in Christ. When his strength was taken away, it was a heavy stroke. And when the strength occasionally returned, he picked up his pen with joy because he did "relish versing."

And now in age I bud again,
After so many deaths I live and write;
I once more smell the dew and rain,
And relish versing: O my onely light,
It cannot be
That I am he
On whom thy tempests fell all night.[57]

---

[55] "Providence," in ibid., 416.
[56] "Dulnesse," in ibid., 410.
[57] "The Flower," in ibid., 568.

He loved to see and savor and speak the saving, restoring power of God. This is what he lived for:

> I live to shew his power, who once did bring
> My *joyes* to *weep*, and now my *griefs* to *sing*.[58]

The Discovery That Saying Leads to Seeing

But Herbert discovered, in his role as the secretary of God's praise, that the poetic effort to speak the riches of God's greatness gave him deeper sight into that greatness. Writing poetry was not merely the expression of his experience with God that he had *before* the writing. The writing was part of the experience of God. It was, in the making, a way of seeing more of God. Deeper communion with God happened *in* the writing. Probably the poem that says this most forcefully is called "The Quidditie"—that is, the essence of things. And his point is that poetic verses are nothing in themselves, but are everything if he is with God in them.

> My God, a verse is not a crown,
> No point of honour, or gay suit,
> No hawk, or banquet, or renown,
> Nor a good sword, nor yet a lute:
>
> It cannot vault, or dance, or play;
> It never was in *France* or *Spain*;
> Nor can it entertain the day
> With a great stable or demain:
>
> It is no office, art, or news;
> Nor the Exchange, or busie Hall;
> But it is that which while I use
> I am with Thee, and *Most take all*.[59]

---

[58] "Josephs Coat," in ibid., 546.

[59] "The Quidditie," in ibid., 253–54. There is little consensus about the meaning of the last phrase: "And Most take all." F. E. Hutchinson gives J. Middleton Murray's explanation: "The titles to esteem, which verse is not, are first detailed; then it is declared that verse nevertheless is the quiddity of them all, in the very real sense that Herbert in his poetry comes nearest to God and most partakes of the creative power that sustains all these excellences." F. E. Hutchinson, *The Works of George Herbert* (Clarendon, 1941), Kindle Edition. Helen Wilcox suggests: "[Most take all] recalls 'Winner takes all' from the card game Primero (a game referred to in *Jordan (I)*); . . . The echo suggests that by giving up worldly interests and trusting in God—as the players give up their cards (and their money) and trust to the luck of

His poems are "that which while I use I am with Thee." Or as Joseph Summers says, "The writing of a verse gave to Herbert 'The Quidditie' of the spiritual experience."[60] Or as Helen Wilcox says, "This phrase makes clear that it is not the finished 'verse' itself which brings the speaker close to God, but the act of 'using' poetry—a process which presumably includes writing, revising, and reading."[61]

"MY UTMOST ART . . . AND CREAM OF ALL MY HEART"

For Herbert, this experience of seeing and savoring God was directly connected with the care and rigor and subtlety and delicacy of his poetic effort—his craft, his art. Thus he says in his poem called "Praise (II)":

> Wherefore with my utmost art
> I will sing thee,
> And the cream of all my heart
> I will bring thee.[62]

The bringing of his *heart* and the singing with utmost *art* are not an incidental rhyme. They are profoundly united in his experience of God. There is, you might say, and ontological rhyme. God himself has established a connection between the "cream of heart" and the "utmost art." To labor in faith to speak the beauty of God in beautiful ways awakens—at least it did for Herbert—the heart's cream of seeing and savoring.

"TO THE ADVANTAGE OF ANY POOR DEJECTED SOUL"

Yet Herbert had in view more than the joys of his own soul as he wrote. He wrote (and dreamed of publishing after death) with a view of serving the church. Pressing in to his "utmost art" and giving form

---

the game—the speaker gains everything. There are thus two winners in the writing of divine poetry: God, and the writer, who 'wins by being won by an omnipotent God' (Nardo 92)." Wilcox, *English Poems of George Herbert*, 255.

[60] Summers, *George Herbert*, 107.
[61] Wilcox, *English Poems of George Herbert*, 255.
[62] "Praise (II)" in ibid., 507.

to "the cream of all [his] heart" was not only for this own soul's joy in God. True, he had never published them during his lifetime, though we know he had been writing seriously for twenty-three years. So they were clearly for his own soul—his way of seeing and savoring the glories of God. But when he came to die, he sent this life collection of poems to his friend Nicholas Ferrar and said, "[If you] can think it may turn to the advantage of any dejected poor soul, let it be made public."[63]

This is, in fact, what he hoped for, because in the introductory poem to the entire collection, he wrote:

> Hearken unto a Verser, who may chance
> Ryme thee to good, and make a bait of pleasure.
>   A verse may finde him, who a sermon flies,
>   And turn delight into a sacrifice.[64]

He believed that the delights he had found in God by writing the poems could become a sacrifice of worship for the reader as well. It may be, he thought, that I can "ryme thee to good."

POETIC EFFORT NOT IN VAIN

And this is, in fact, what has happened. People have met God in Herbert's poems, and their lives have been changed. Joseph Summers said of Herbert's poems, "We can only recognize . . . the immediate imperative of the greatest art: 'You must change your life.'"[65] Simone Weil, the French philosopher was totally agnostic toward God and Christianity but encountered Herbert's poem "Love (III)" and became a kind of Christian mystic,[66] calling this poem "the most beautiful poem in the world."[67]

LOVE (III)

Love bade me welcome: yet my soul drew back,
   Guiltie of dust and sinne.

---

[63] Walton, *The Life of Mr. George Herbert*, in Tobin, *George Herbert*, 311.
[64] "The Church-porch," in Wilcox, *English Poems of George Herbert*, 50.
[65] Summers, *George Herbert*, 190.
[66] Falloon, *Heart in Pilgrimage*, 200.
[67] Wilcox, *English Poems of George Herbert*, xxi.

But quick-ey'd Love, observing me grow slack
        From my first entrance in,
Drew nearer to me, sweetly questioning
        If I lack'd any thing.

A guest, I answer'd, worthy to be here:
        Love said, you shall be he.
I the unkinde, ungratefull? Ah my deare,
        I cannot look on thee.
Love took my hand, and smiling did reply,
        Who made the eyes but I?

Truth Lord, but I have marr'd them: let my shame
        Go where it doth deserve.
And know you not, sayes Love, who bore the blame?
        My deare, then I will serve.
You must sit down, sayes Love, and taste my meat:
        So I did sit and eat.[68]

It is a beautiful poem. Beautiful in form and beautiful in substance. It is the poem Herbert apparently chose to close the entire collection of his life's work. In that position, at the end of *The Temple*, it takes on a climactic resolution and peacefulness.

He had told his friend Nicholas Ferrar shortly before his death that in this collection of poems, which were his life's work, he would find "a picture of the many spiritual conflicts that have passed betwixt God and my soul." But then he added, "Before I could subject mine to the will of Jesus my Master, in whose service I have now found perfect freedom." This final, peaceful subjection and freedom is the spirit of this concluding poem in *The Temple*, "Love (III)."

Chana Bloch argues that "Love (III)" "contains *The Temple* in brief" proceeding "by a series of careful balancings . . . until it comes to rest in the last line emphatically on the side of God's love."[69] Gene Veith says similarly, "The final poem . . . is the capstone of *The Temple*, recapitulating and resolving once and for all the paradoxes of sin and grace, guilt and love, that are Herbert's continual themes. . . . The feast por-

---

[68] "Love (III)," in ibid., 661.
[69] Quoted in ibid., 660.

trayed in 'Love (III)' is the goal of all the preceding poems."[70] Indeed, Veith circles back to what we saw earlier and says, "Just as there are few religious poems so positive or joyful in their message and in their effects, so there are few poems that are so Calvinistic."[71]

RELIEF AND BUOYANCY: THE CHARACTERISTIC NOTES

Again we must recall what C. S. Lewis reminded us of earlier about the early Calvinist of Herbert's day:

> Like an accepted lover, he feels that he has done nothing, and never could have done anything, to deserve such astonishing happiness. . . . His own puny and ridiculous efforts would be as helpless to retain the joy as they would have been to achieve it in the first place. . . . Relief and buoyancy are the characteristic notes.[72]
>
> [This kind of Protestantism] was not too grim, but too glad, to be true.[73]

In other words, one of the marks of this Calvinism was that God's sovereign self-exaltation was supremely expressed in preventing man from putting God in the place of a dependent master who needs servants to sustain him. Instead God expresses his sovereignty in putting humble and dependent man finally and permanently where God will serve him with the inexhaustible resources of the riches of his glory. Hence the last lines of Herbert's poem and Herbert's life work:

> And know you not, sayes Love, who bore the blame?
> My deare, then I will serve.
> You must sit down, sayes Love, and taste my meat:
> So I did sit and eat.[74]

Herbert protests that he will return God the favor of bearing his blame: "My deare, then I will serve." But this Lover will not have it. "Nor is he

---

[70] Veith, *Reformation Spirituality*, 171–72.
[71] Ibid.
[72] Lewis, *Poetry and Prose*, 33–34.
[73] Ibid.
[74] "Love (III)," in Wilcox, *English Poems of George Herbert*, 661.

served by human hands, as though he needed anything, since he himself gives to all mankind life and breath and everything" (Acts 17:25).
"The Son of Man came not to be served but to serve, and to give his
life as a ransom for many" (Mark 10:45). No, eternity will not be spent
with human beings paying back the debt of grace we owe. Grace that
can be paid back is not grace. Rather, for all eternity, we will be the
beneficiaries of God's kindness. This Lover saves us so that "in the
coming ages he might show the immeasurable riches of his grace in
kindness toward us in Christ Jesus" (Ephesians 2:7).

> You must sit down, sayes Love, and taste my meat:
> So I did sit and eat.[75]

This is the end of the matter. No more striving. No more struggle. No
more "spiritual conflicts [passing] betwixt God and my soul." Instead,
Love himself serves the poet's soul as he sits and receives.

LOVE'S YOKE IS EASY

This is not the excess of a poet's imagination. This is the dream come
true of a poet whose mind is saturated with the Bible. You might say
that these last lines are a lucid echo of the promise of Jesus in Luke
12:37. Jesus portrays his second coming as the return of a master who,
instead of demanding service, serves:

> Blessed are those servants whom the master finds awake when he
> comes. Truly, I say to you, he will dress himself for service and have
> them recline at table, and he will come and serve them.

Herbert has struggled all his life to know that Love's yoke is easy and
its burden is light. He had come to find that this is true. And he ended
his poems and his life with the most astonishing expression of it in all
the Bible: The King of kings will "dress himself for service and have
them recline at table, and he will come and serve them."

> You must sit down, sayes Love, and taste my meat:
> So I did sit and eat.[76]

---

[75] Ibid.
[76] Ibid.

A Pearl That Cost Him the World

Herbert hoped that the record of his own encounters with God in his poetry would do good to others. And they have. God had brought him through so many afflictions and so many temptations that his poems bore the marks not only of his "utmost art"[77] but also of utmost reality. Sitting finally in peace at his Master's table did not come without the temptations of all that the world had to offer—the lure of academia, the pull of political power, the raw pleasures of the body that are open to such positions—he had known access to them all.

His poem called "The Pearle" includes in the title "Matth. 13." It's a reference to Matthew 13:45–46, "The kingdom of heaven is like a merchant in search of fine pearls, who, on finding one pearl of great value, went and sold all that he had and bought it." The poem unfolds Herbert's experience of the world and how he came to purchase the pearl.

> I know the wayes of *learning*; both the head
> And pipes that feed the presse, and make it runne;
> . . .
>
> I know the wayes of *honour*, what maintains
> The quick returns of courtesie and wit:
> . . .
>
> I know the wayes of *pleasure*, the sweet strains,
> The lullings and the relishes of it;
> . . .
>
> I know all these, and have them in my hand.
> Therefore not sealed, but with open eyes
> I fly to thee, and fully understand
> Both the main sale, and the commodities;
> And at what rate and price I have thy love; . . .[78]

"Weariness May Toss Him to My Breast"

He had found, at last, satisfaction and rest in Christ not because he didn't know any alternatives but because he knew them well and

---

[77] "Praise (II)" in ibid., 507.
[78] "The Pearle. *Matth. 13*" in ibid., 322–23 (emphasis mine).

found that they were not enough. One of his most famous poems, "The Pulley," describes how God himself gave wonderful gifts in this world but plotted to protect man from idolatry by withholding rest.

THE PULLEY

When God at first made man,
Having a glasse of blessings standing by;
Let us (said he) poure on him all we can:
Let the worlds riches, which dispersed lie,
Contract into a span.

So strength first made a way;
Then beautie flow'd, then wisdome, honour, pleasure:
When almost all was out, God made a stay,
Perceiving that alone of all his treasure
Rest in the bottome lay.

For if I should (said he)
Bestow this jewell also on my creature,
He would adore my gifts in stead of me,
And rest in Nature, not the God of Nature:
So both should losers be.

Yet let him keep the rest,
But keep them with repining restlesnesse:
Let him be rich and wearie, that at least,
If goodnesse leade him not, yet wearinesse
May tosse him to my breast.[79]

"GUILDED CLAY"

Beauty, wisdom, honor, pleasure—good gifts of God, but O so dangerous. Herbert tasted them both ways. And found, by the sovereign grace of God, that restlessness would finally toss him to his Master's breast and seat him at his Master's table. God granted the miracle of the human heart—to see before it is too late that this world, without God, is "guilded clay." Hence his poem "Frailtie" begins,

---

[79] "The Pulley," in ibid., 548–49.

Lord, in my silence how do I despise
>>What upon trust
Is styled *honour, riches,* or *fair eyes*;
>>But is *fair dust*!
I surname them *guilded clay,*
>>*Deare earth, fine grasse* or *hay*;
In all, I think my foot doth ever tread
>>Upon their head.

But even in this poem that begins so confidently, the conflict between God and his soul breaks out again:

But when I view abroad both Regiments;
>>The worlds, and thine:
Thine clad with simplenesse, and sad events;
>>The other fine,
Full of glorie and gay weeds,
>>Brave language, braver deeds:
That which was dust before, doth quickly rise,
>>And prick mine eyes.

O brook not this, lest if what even now
>>My foot did tread,
Affront those joyes, wherewith thou didst endow
>>And long since wed
My poore soul, ev'n sick of love:
>>It may a Babel prove
Commodious to conquer heav'n and thee
>>Planted in me.[80]

"That which was dust before [in stanza one!], doth quickly rise, and prick mine eyes." The world, that was unattractive in one moment rises up and lures his eyes again. So he pleads with God. "O brook not this." Don't let this happen. Forbid it. Just now my foot was treading on the "gay weeds" of this world's temptations. O let them not rise up and prove to be a Tower of Babel in me rising up to oppose heaven and God himself.

---

[80] "Frailtie," in ibid., 260.

THE TRIUMPH OF SEEING AND SAYING DIVINE BEAUTY

So when Herbert finally came to rest from the battle and take his seat at the Master's table, it was not because there were no powerful conflicts. He had known them, fought them, and won them. And among his weapons of his triumph were both the *seeing* and the *saying* of divine beauty. The power of knowing God and the poetic effort of showing God had won the day.

Thus George Herbert's impact as a poet was owing to his deep Reformed spirituality—that is, his proven theology of grace, centered on the cross—and to the conflicts of his soul that brought him through the lures of the world to the love of Christ, and to his poetic effort to express all this with his "utmost art" and the "cream of all his heart."[81]

A MODEST PROPOSAL: POETIC EFFORT

In keeping with the focus of this book, I will close this chapter with an exhortation for everyone who is called to speak about great things. I think that includes everyone—at least everyone who has been called out of darkness by Jesus Christ. "But you are . . . a people for his own possession, *that you may proclaim the excellencies of him who called you* out of darkness into his marvelous light" (1 Peter 2:9). Every Christian is called to speak of God's excellencies.

My exhortation is that it would be fruitful for your own soul, and for the people you speak to, if you also made a *poetic effort* to see and savor and show the glories of Christ. I don't mean the effort to write poetry. Very few are called to do that. I mean the effort to see and savor and show the glories of Christ by giving some prayerful effort to finding striking, penetrating, and awakening ways of saying the excellencies that we see.

COLLECTING PROVERBS AS POETIC EFFORT

There are two little-appreciated habits of George Herbert that point to the kind of poetic effort for nonpoets that I am commending. First, Herbert collected proverbs. These were first published in 1640 in the

---

[81] "Praise (II)," in ibid., 507.

periodical *Witts Recreation*, under the title: "Outlandish Proverbs Selected by Mr. G. H." Most of them were translations of proverbs from French, Spanish, and Italian sources. That's why they were called "Outlandish Proverbs," which simply meant, at that time, *outside our own land*, that is, *foreign*. There were at least 1,184 of these proverbs, which are available today in F. E. Hutchinson's *The Works of George Herbert*.

Collecting proverbs was not an unusual practice at the time. We know, for example, that Francis Bacon, Erasmus, and two of Herbert's brothers collected proverbs. Herbert's collection included sayings like:

2. He begins to die, that quits his desires.

12. A good bargain is a pick-purse.

13. The scalded dog fears cold water.

14. Pleasing ware is half sold.

35. He loses nothing, that loses not God.

199. I wept when I was borne, and every day shows why.

258. I had rather ride on an ass that carries me, than a horse that throws me.

456. Good finds good.

698. Though you see a Church-man ill, yet continue in the Church still.

769. One foot is better then two crutches.

1059. Heresy may be easier kept out, than shook off.

1074. Two sparrows on one Ear of Corn make an ill agreement.

1121. We must recoil a little, to the end we may leap the better.

1122. No love is foul, nor prison fair.

1159. A man is known to be mortal by two things, Sleep and Lust.

1174. Civil Wars of France made a million of Atheists, and thirty thousand Witches.

1182. Money wants no followers.

LANGUAGE THAT STRIKES HOME

Jane Falloon gives one explanation of Herbert's practice of collecting such proverbs:

> He showed a delight in them, and used them in his poems, especially in the long poem "The Sacrifice," in which many of the verses contain a proverb. Herbert must have collected them as other

people collect stamps or matchboxes: a light-hearted hobby with underlying gleams of seriousness, in the succinct wisdom so many of them hold.[82]

I agree. But I would add this. Herbert was committed to speaking of the glories of Christ with language that struck home. Part of his poetic effort was to understand why certain ways of saying things had attained proverbial status. Why do these words strike and stick? And his aim was to form the habit of speaking and writing with this pungency.

When you read Herbert's poems, you can see the effect of the pithy, epigrammatic influence of proverbial diction. Some of the proverbs are manifestly poetic: "No love is foul, nor prison fair." Others are shrewd: "Pleasing ware is half sold." Others are humorously illuminating: "The scalded dog fears cold water." Others are profound: "He loses nothing, that loses not God." And all of them bear the kind of short, sharp, compact, aphoristic mark that we find in so many of Herbert's poems. For example, his line: "While all things have their will, yet none but thine."[83] Or: "A verse may find him, who a sermon flies."[84] Or: "Beauty and beauteous words should go together."[85] Or: "What Adam had, and forfeited for all, Christ keepeth now, who cannot fail or fall."[86]

So my point is this: Whether you aim to write poetry or not, there are things you can do that make your speech more savory, more compelling, more like the point of Proverbs 25:11: "A word fitly spoken is like apples of gold in a setting of silver." Or Proverbs 15:23: "To make an apt answer is a joy to a man, and a word in season, how good it is!"

THE POETIC EFFORT OF LOVING MUSIC

I mentioned that there were two habits Herbert had which were part of his poetic effort. One was collecting proverbs. The other was the pursuit and enjoyment of music. He was an accomplished lutenist and played the viol. About a fourth of his poems refer to music.[87] He said once, "Music points the way to heaven as it frees us, for the moment,

---

[82] Falloon, *Heart in Pilgrimage*, 53.
[83] "Providence," Wilcox, *English Poems of George Herbert*, 417.
[84] "The Church-porch," in ibid., 50.
[85] "Forerunners," in ibid., 612.
[86] "The Holdfast," in ibid., 499.
[87] Summers, *George Herbert*, 157.

from the limitations of our bodily being and gives us strength back to believe in final harmony."[88] His earliest biographer wrote:

> His chiefest recreation was Music, in which heavenly art he was a most excellent master, and did himself compose many Divine Hymns and Anthems, which he set and sang to his lute or viol: and though he was a lover of retiredness, yet his love of Music was such, that he went usually twice every week, on certain appointed days, to the Cathedral Church in Salisbury; and at his return would say "that his time spent in prayer, and Cathedral-music elevated his soul, and was his Heaven upon earth."[89]

It seems to me that for Herbert, music functioned to shape both the source and the style of his poetry. By source, I mean his soul. If the soul has no harmony, the mind will have no poetry. Music shaped his soul and put him in a frame of mind that could see and savor beauty. And music shaped his style. He is lyrical. His poems don't just say; they sing. There is a musical flow.

So music was part of Herbert's poetic effort. That is, it was a part of his life that contributed to the compelling way he spoke and wrote. Whether it is in collecting pungent proverbs or loving beautiful music, there are ways to enrich and refine and sharpen the penetrating power of your language. This is part of what I mean by poetic effort.

SAYING AS A WAY OF SEEING

For Herbert, these habits supported the main path of seeing and savoring the beauty of Christ—the path of writing poetry. This path was not only a way of saying but a way of seeing. What I am proposing is that Herbert's effort to write with unusual poetic power was a way of meditating on the glories of Christ. I am suggesting that poetic effort is a fruitful means of meditation.

In this, I'm proposing one answer (among many) to the question: What does it mean to meditate on the excellencies—the glories—of Christ? What ways has God given us for lingering over the glory-laden Word of God until that glory is seen and savored in our minds and

---

[88] Magee, *George Herbert*, 23.
[89] Falloon, *Heart in Pilgrimage*, 48.

hearts in a way that is worthy of its supreme value? What steps can we take to help us fruitfully meditate on the glory of Christ until we see?

Of course, one essential biblical answer is to pray. Pray prayers like, "Open my eyes, that I may behold wondrous things" (Psalm 119:18). Or as Paul prays, "[Have] the eyes of our hearts enlightened" (Ephesians 1:18). We often fail to see glory because we don't earnestly ask to see it.

But then what? Suppose you have prayed earnestly for God to open the eyes of your heart so that ordinary words in the Bible become radiant with glory, beauty, and excellence. Now what? After we have asked God to do his part, what is our part? Through what human means does God intend to do his part? The answer I am proposing in this book is this: *poetic effort*. And the conviction behind it is this: *The effort to say freshly is a way of seeing freshly. The effort to say strikingly is a way of seeing strikingly. The effort to say beautifully is a way of seeing beauty.* And you don't have to write poetry to make this "poetic" effort.

For George Herbert, poetry was a form of mediation on the glories of Christ mediated through the Scriptures. Conceiving and writing poems was a way of holding a glimpse of divine glory in his mind and turning it around and around until it yielded an opening into some aspect of its essence or its wonder that he had never seen before—or felt.

This is meditation: Getting glimpses of glory in the Bible or in the world and turning those glimpses around and around in your mind, looking and looking. And for Herbert, this effort to *see* and *savor* the glory of Christ was the effort to *say* it as it had never been said before.

The Greatest Example of Turning the Diamond

One of the best examples of Herbert's meditation on a single glory by turning it around and around before his eyes is his poem on the glorious reality of prayer. My guess is that when you read my phrase "glorious reality of prayer," you feel a disconnect between my big language and your small experience of prayer. Yes. So do I. But just a moment's reflection and you realize, prayer is glorious. How could talking to the Creator of the universe personally not be glorious? How could something not be glorious that cost the Son of God his life, so that sinners may come boldly to a throne, not of judgment, but of grace. Herbert

tasted this glory, and he wanted to see more. So he turned this dia-
mond around and around. Read Herbert's meditation on prayer slowly.

PRAYER (I)

Prayer the Churches banquet, Angels age,
    Gods breath in man returning to his birth,
    The soul in paraphrase, heart in pilgrimage,
The Christian plummet sounding heav'n and earth;

Engine against th' Almightie, sinners towre,
    Reversed thunder, Christ-side-piercing spear,
    The six-daies world transposing in an houre,
A kinde of tune, which all things heare and fear;

Softnesse, and peace, and joy, and love, and blisse,
    Exalted Manna, gladnesse of the best,
    Heaven in ordinarie, man well drest,
The milkie way, the bird of Paradise,

    Church-bels beyond the starres heard, the souls bloud,
    The land of spices; something understood.[90]

Twenty-five images of prayer. My favorite is "reversed thunder." Think
of it! Where did these pictures, these images, these words, come from?
They came from long, focused, prayerful, Bible-saturated brooding over
a single glorious reality. They came from humble, prayerful *poetic effort*.
Before this effort, prayer was a word. Perhaps a wonderful word. Perhaps
a rich experience. But now, on this side of the poetic effort, prayer is
seen to be more than we ever dreamed. Herbert *saw* as he labored to *say*.

PUTTING INTO WORDS AS A WAY OF SEEING WORTH

Herbert found, as most poets have, that the effort to put the glimpse
of glory into striking or moving words makes the glimpse grow. The
effort to say deeply what he saw made the seeing deeper. The effort to
put the wonder in an unexpected rhyme, a pleasing rhythm, a startling
cadence or meter, an uncommon metaphor, a surprising expression,

---

[90] "Prayer (I)," in Wilcox, *English Poems of George Herbert*, 178.

an unusual juxtaposition, or in words that blend agreeably with assonance or consonance—all this effort (I'm calling it *poetic effort* quite apart from poem writing) caused his heart's eyes to see the wonder in new ways. *The poetic effort to say beautifully was a way of seeing beauty.* The effort to find worthy words for Christ opens to us more fully the worth of Christ—and the *experience* of the worth of Christ. As Herbert says of his own poetic effort: "It is that which, while I use, I am with thee."[91]

My point of application is that this can be true for all of us—all those who have tasted and seen that the Lord is good. All who have been called out of darkness into the light of marvelous realities— "unsearchable riches of Christ" (Ephesians 3:8). Preachers have this job supremely. But all of us, Peter says, are called out of darkness to "proclaim the excellencies" (1 Peter 2:9). When we were converted to Christ, we were thrown into an ocean of wonder. In this life, we are to get a start on the eternity we will spend going deeper and higher into the "unsearchable riches." And my point here for all of us is *the effort to put the excellencies into worthy words is a way of seeing the worth of the excellencies. The effort to say more about the glory than you have ever said is a way of seeing more than you have ever seen.*

Poetry is a pointer to this. What poetry emphasizes—poetry from George Herbert and poetry throughout the Bible—is that the effort to say it surprisingly and provocatively and beautifully uncovers truth and beauty that you may not find any other way. I say it carefully. I do not claim that poetic effort is a *necessary* way of seeing a facet of Christ's beauty. God may open our eyes by other means—by some act of obedience, by hard study, by watching the mountains, by the gift of your own cancer, or by the death of your spouse or your child. But the poetic effort *is* a way—a pervasively biblical way, a historically proven way—of seeing and savoring and showing the glory of God.

Therefore, I commend it to you. And I commend one of its greatest patrons, the poet-pastor, George Herbert.

---

[91] See note 59 on the poem "Quidditie." His poem, "Prayer," is one of the clearest examples of the fruit of lingering over a glory—in this case the glory of prayer—and seeing the wonders of it by the poetic effort to say it in ways it had never been said before.

Hail, happy Saint, on thine immortal throne!
To thee complaints of grievance are unknown;
We hear no more the music of thy tongue,
Thy wonted auditories cease to throng.
Thy lessons in unequal'd accents flow'd!
While emulation in each bosom glow'd;
Thou didst, in strains of eloquence refin'd,
Inflame the soul, and captivate the mind.
Unhappy we, the setting Sun deplore!
Which once was splendid, but it shines no more;
He leaves this earth for Heav'n's unmeasur'd height;
And worlds unknown, receive him from our sight.
There WHITEFIELD wings, with rapid course his way,
And sails to Zion, through vast seas of day.

Phillis Wheatley

2

"I WILL NOT BE A VELVET-MOUTHED PREACHER!"

The Life and Eloquence of George Whitefield

The facts about George Whitefield's preaching as an eighteenth-century itinerant evangelist are almost unbelievable. Can they really be true? Judging by multiple attestations of his contemporaries—and by the agreement of sympathetic and unsympathetic biographers—they seem to be so.

From his first outdoor sermon on February 17, 1739, at the age of twenty-four, to the coal miners of Kingswood near Bristol, England, until his death thirty years later on September 30, 1770, in Newburyport, Massachusetts (where he is buried), his life was one of almost daily preaching. Sober estimates are that he spoke about one thousand times every year for thirty years. That included at least eighteen thousand sermons and twelve thousand talks and exhortations.[1]

SPEAKING MORE THAN SLEEPING

The daily pace he kept for thirty years meant that many weeks he was speaking more than he was sleeping. Henry Venn, vicar of Hud-

---

[1] Michael A. G. Haykin, ed., *The Revived Puritan: The Spirituality of George Whitefield* (Dundas, Ontario: Joshua, 2000), 32–33. Arnold Dallimore, *George Whitefield: The Life and Times of the Great Evangelist of the Eighteenth-Century Revival* (Edinburgh: Banner of Truth, 1970), 2:522.

dersfield, who knew Whitefield well, expressed amazement for us all when he wrote,

> Who would think it possible that a person . . . should speak in the compass of a single week (and that for years) in general forty hours, and in very many, sixty, and that to thousands; and after this labor, instead of taking any rest, should be offering up prayers and intercessions, with hymns and spiritual songs, as his manner was, in every house to which he was invited.[2]

Make sure you hear that accurately. Many weeks he was actually speaking (not preparing to speak, which he had virtually no time to do) for *sixty* hours (60, not 16). On the slower weeks, that's almost six hours a day, seven days a week, and on the heavier weeks, over eight hours a day.

Preaching, Preaching, Preaching

In all of my reading about Whitefield, I have found no references to what we today would call *vacations* or *days off*. When he thought he needed recuperation, he spoke of an ocean voyage to America. He crossed the Atlantic thirteen times in his life—an odd number (not even) because he died and was buried in America, not in England. The trips across the Atlantic took eight to ten weeks each. That's about two years of his life in a boat! And even though he preached virtually every day on the ship,[3] the pace was different, and he was able to read and write and rest.[4]

But on land, the preaching pace was unremitting. Two years before he died at the age of fifty-five, he wrote in a letter, "I love the open bracing air." And the following year, he said, "It is good to go into the highways and hedges. Field-preaching, field-preaching forever!"[5] Day after day all his life, he went everywhere preaching, preaching, preaching.

---

[2] J. I. Packer, "The Spirit with the Word: The Reformational Revivalism of George Whitefield," in *Honouring the People of God, The Collected Shorter Writings of J. I. Packer* (Carlisle, UK: Paternoster, 1999), 4:40.
[3] Harry S. Stout, *The Divine Dramatist: George Whitfield and the Rise of Modern Evangelicalism* (Grand Rapids, MI: Eerdmans, 1991), 59.
[4] Dallimore, *George Whitefield*, 2:284.
[5] Haykin, *Revived Puritan*, 30.

Speaking to Thousands

And keep in mind that most of these messages were spoken to gatherings of thousands of people—usually in difficulties of wind and competing noise. For example, in the fall of 1740, for over a month he preached almost every day in New England to crowds of up to eight thousand people. That was when the population of Boston, the largest city in the region, was not much larger than that.[6]

He recounts that in Philadelphia that same year on Wednesday, April 6, he preached on Society Hill twice in the morning to about six thousand and in the evening to nearly eight thousand. On Thursday, he spoke to "upwards of ten thousand," and it was reported at one of these events that his expression of the text, "He opened his mouth and taught them saying," was distinctly heard at Gloucester point, a distance of two miles by water down the Delaware River.[7] Do you see why I say such things are nearly unbelievable? And there were times when the crowds reached twenty thousand or more.[8] This meant that the physical exertion to project his voice to that many people for so long, in each sermon, for so many times every week, for thirty years, was Herculean.[9]

One Scarcely Interrupted Sermon

Add to this the fact that he was continually traveling, in a day when it was done by horse or carriage or ship. He covered the length and breadth of England repeatedly. He regularly traveled and spoke throughout Wales. He visited Ireland twice, where he was almost killed by a mob from which he carried a scar on his forehead for the rest of his life.[10] He traveled fourteen times to Scotland and came to America seven times, stopping once in Bermuda for eleven weeks—all for preaching, not resting. He preached in virtually every major town on the Eastern Seaboard of America. Michael Haykin reminds us, "What is so remark-

---

[6] Mark Noll, *The Old Religion in a New World: The History of North American Christianity* (Grand Rapids, MI: Eerdmans, 2002), 52.
[7] Dallimore, *Whitefield*, 1:480.
[8] Haykin, *Revived Puritan*, 31–32.
[9] Once when I was speaking to about two hundred people outdoors on a windy day, the generator for the sound system died. I finished my message for maybe fifteen minutes trying to be heard, and found it to be a strain. That was two hundred, not two thousand.
[10] Stout, *Divine Dramatist*, 209.

able about all of this is that Whitefield lived at a time when travel to a town but 20 miles away was a significant undertaking."[11]

J. C. Ryle summed up Whitefield's life like this:

> The facts of Whitefield's history . . . are almost entirely of one complexion. One year was just like another; and to attempt to follow him would be only going repeatedly over the same ground. From 1739 to the year of his death, 1770, a period of 31 years, his life was one uniform employment. He was eminently a man of one thing, and always about his Master's business. From Sunday mornings to Saturday nights, from 1 January to 31 December, excepting when laid aside by illness, he was almost incessantly preaching Christ and going about the world entreating men to repent and come to Christ and be saved.[12]

Another nineteenth-century biographer said, "His whole life may be said to have been consumed in the delivery of one continuous, or scarcely interrupted sermon."[13]

A PHENOMENON IN CHURCH HISTORY

He was a phenomenon not just of his age but in the entire two-thousand-year history of Christian preaching. There has been nothing like the combination of his preaching pace and geographic extent and auditory scope and attention-holding effect and converting power. Ryle is right: "No preacher has ever retained his hold on his hearers so entirely as he did for thirty-four years. His popularity never waned."[14]

His contemporary Augustus Toplady (1740–1778) remembered him as "the apostle of the English Empire."[15] He was "Anglo America's most popular eighteenth-century preacher and its first truly mass revivalist."[16] He was "the first colonial-American religious celebrity."[17] Eight years of his life were spent in America. He loved the American ethos. He was more American in his blood, it seems, than he was English.

---

[11] Haykin, *Revived Puritan*, 33.
[12] J. C. Ryle, *Select Sermons of George Whitefield: With an Account of His Life* (Edinburgh: Banner of Truth, 1958), 21–22.
[13] Dallimore, *George Whitefield*, 2:522.
[14] Ryle, *Select Sermons of George Whitefield*, 32.
[15] Augustus Toplady quoted in Haykin, *Revived Puritan*, 23.
[16] Stout, *Divine Dramatist*, xiii.
[17] Ibid., 92.

AMERICA'S FIRST CELEBRITY

Harry Stout points out, "As tensions between England and America grew [Whitefield] saw he might have to choose. Wesley would remain loyal to England, and Whitefield could not. His institutional attachments and personal identification with the colonies were stronger than his loyalty to the crown."[18]

Estimates are that 80 percent of the entire population of the American colonies (this is before TV or radio) heard Whitefield at least once. Stout shows that Whitefield's impact on America was such that

> he can justly be styled America's first cultural hero. Before Whitefield, there was no unifying inter-colonial person or event. Indeed, before Whitefield, it is doubtful any name other than royalty was known equally from Boston to Charleston. But by 1750 virtually every American loved and admired Whitefield and saw him as their champion.[19]

William Cowper who died when Whitefield was twenty-nine already called him "the wonder of the age."[20]

PREACHING WAS EVERYTHING

This was all the effect of the most single-minded, oratorically enthralling, thunder-voiced devotion to daily evangelistic preaching that history has ever known. Preaching was everything. Perhaps most of his biographers would agree that Whitefield, to quote Stout,

> demonstrated a callous disregard for his private self, both body and spirit. The preaching moment engulfed all, and it would continue to do so, for in fact there was nothing else he lived for. . . . The private man and the family man had long since ceased to exist. In the final scene, there was only Whitefield in his pulpit.[21]

Howell Harris was one of Whitefield's closest friends—at least in his early ministry. Harris introduced Whitefield to open-air preaching,

---

[18] Ibid., 261.
[19] Harry S. Stout, "Heavenly Comet," *Christian History*, 38 (1993), 13–14.
[20] Haykin, *Revived Puritan*, 23.
[21] Stout, *Divine Dramatist*, 276–77.

taught him courage in the pulpit, and later found him a wife. Before Harris introduced Whitefield to the widow Elizabeth James, Whitefield had been rejected by Elizabeth Delamotte, whom he had proposed to in a letter from America in 1740. From this letter, we get a sense of how pragmatic Whitefield was about marriage. He emphasized not a romantic attraction to her but his need for help, for example with his "increasing family" of orphans. He wrote,

> You need not be afraid of sending me a refusal. For, I bless God, if I know anything of my own heart, I am free from that foolish passion which the world calls *Love*. . . . The passionate expressions which carnal courtiers use, I think, ought to be avoided by those that would marry in the Lord. . . . I trust, I love you only for God, and desire to be joined to you only by his command and for his sake.[22]

That Elizabeth rejected the proposal. The other Elizabeth had been a widow for ten years; she was neither pretty nor much attracted to Whitefield. But Harris persuaded them both that the union would be good. They were married on November 14, 1741, in Abergavenny, South Wales. In a letter to Gilbert Tennent, Whitefield mentioned his marriage: "About 11 weeks ago I married, in the fear of God, one who was a widow, of about 36 years of age, and has been a housekeeper for many years; neither rich in fortune, nor beautiful as to her person, but, I believe, a true child of God."[23]

After two years, they had a son named John. He died in infancy, even though Whitefield had had a strong impression that he would be a great preacher. Elizabeth endured four miscarriages, but they remained childless. They were often separated for months at a time, and from February 1747 to June 1749, she remained in America while he was away. There was never any fear or accusation of unfaithfulness, as both of them were committed to the highest standards of sexual faithfulness. But the marriage seemed more functional than amorous.

On August 9, 1768, Elizabeth died after twenty-seven years of marriage to Whitefield. Whatever grief he felt was consumed in the passion for evangelism. He wrote only days after her death, "Let us

---

[22] Ibid., 167.
[23] Ibid., 170.

work whilst it is day."[24] Two weeks later he was preparing to leave for America again.

Whitefield's marriage, like John Wesley's, was not the model of wholeness. Surely this is in part because Whitefield himself was the fruit of a very broken family. His father died when he was two leaving a widow, an inn, and seven children. Eight years later his mother married Capel Longden, who tried to get the inn for himself, and failing, deserted the family.[25] Thus Whitefield grew up not only without a father but with a very poor example in the one father figure he briefly knew. This is not to excuse the emotional distance he felt from Elizabeth. But it is valuable to know some of the roots of the imperfections of our fallible heroes.

Natural and Spiritual Power

What shall we make of the public phenomenon of George Whitefield? What was the key to his power? Asking this question leads us into issues similar to what we saw in the ministry of George Herbert. Herbert's poetic effort focused on the making of poems. Whitefield's poetic effort focused on the making of sermons. And I don't mean the writing of sermons but the astonishing moment of delivering sermons. When I say *poetic effort*, I mean the entire energy of mind and soul and body that created, in the electrifying moment of preaching, something more than just intelligible words transmitting information. Specific biblical passages and doctrines were chosen, and specific words, sequences, consonances, assonances, cadences, images, narratives, characters, tones, pathoses, gestures, movements, facial expressions—all combined for an astonishing impact on believer and unbeliever alike.

Just as Herbert's poetry is studied and admired by many who do not share his faith in Christ and do not use his poetry the way he hoped they would, so also Whitefield's oratory was admired and studied then, as it is now, by people who did not share his faith and who did not respond to his messages the way he prayed they would. Therefore, in the case of George Whitefield, as with George Herbert, we must face the issue of how the natural and supernatural intersect in his poetic effort.

---

[24] Ibid., 267.
[25] Ibid., 2.

At one level, Whitefield's power was the natural power of eloquence, and at another it was the spiritual power of God to convert
sinners and transform communities. There is no reason to doubt that
he was the instrument of God in the salvation of thousands. J. C.
Ryle said,

> I believe that the direct good which he did to immortal souls was
> enormous. I will go further—I believe it is incalculable. Credible
> witnesses in England, Scotland, and America have placed on record
> their conviction that he was the means of converting thousands
> of people.[26]

The Bible makes clear that true conversion to Christ is not a merely
natural event. It is not mere information, argument, emotion, and
words connecting persuasively with someone's brain and altering the
way they think and feel about Jesus. True conversion is a miracle of
new birth, or new creation, brought about by the Spirit of God through
the message of the gospel. There is an intersection of natural and supernatural. Without the supernatural, the "natural man" would never
be converted, Paul says, "The natural person does not accept the things
of the Spirit of God, for they are folly to him, and he is not able to
understand them because they are spiritually discerned" (1 Corinthians
2:14). The only way the "natural person" can be brought to see and
believe is for God to act supernaturally: "I planted, Apollos watered,
but God gave the growth" (1 Corinthians 3:6).

When a rich man turned away from Jesus, he said, "It is easier
for a camel to go through the eye of a needle than for a rich person to enter the kingdom of God" (Mark 10:25). When his disciples
asked, "Then who can be saved?" Jesus said, "With man it is impos-
sible, but not with God. For all things are possible with God" (Mark
10:26–27). Yes, and *only* possible with God. How does the New Testament say that?

- When Peter confessed Christ as the Son of God, Jesus said, "Flesh
  and blood has not revealed this to you, but my Father who is in
  heaven" (Matthew 16:17).

---

[26] Ryle, *Select Sermons of George Whitefield*, 28.

- When Lydia believed on Christ, Luke explains the conversion like this: "The Lord opened her heart to pay attention to what was said by Paul" (Acts 16:14).
- When Paul explained how unbelievers cease to be blinded by the Devil to the glory of Christ in the gospel, he said, "God, who said, 'Let light shine out of darkness,' has shone in our hearts to give the light of the knowledge of the glory of God in the face of Jesus Christ" (2 Corinthians 4:6).
- When Peter explains this miracle he says that it happens through the preaching of the gospel: "You have been born again, not of perishable seed but of imperishable, through the living and abiding word of God; . . . And this word is the good news that was preached to you" (1 Peter 1:23–25).
- Similarly James says that the miracle of being born of God comes by the Word: "Of his own will he brought us forth by the word of truth" (James 1:18).

So the Bible and the witnesses of his own day combine to testify that Whitefield's converts were not merely the product of natural talent or oratory. Many of them were truly born of God—supernaturally changed. This was true of the wider movement of the day called the Great Awakening. Real conversions by supernatural means were happening, but they were happening through real flesh-and-blood people preaching sermons with both poetic effort and supernatural anointing.

Whitefield was the main international instrument of God in this first Great Awakening. No one else in the eighteenth century was anointed like this in America and England and Wales and Scotland and Ireland. This preaching was not a flash in the pan. Deep and lasting things happened.

HIS EFFECT ON EDWARDS AND WILBERFORCE

In February of 1740, Jonathan Edwards sent an invitation to Whitefield in Georgia asking him to come preach in his church. On October 19, Whitefield recorded in his journal, "Preached this morning, and good Mr. Edwards wept during the whole time of exercise. The people were equally affected."[27] Edwards reported that the effect of Whitefield's

---

[27] Dallimore, *George Whitefield*, 1:538.

ministry was more than momentary—"In about a month there was a great alteration in the town."[28]

The impact of Whitefield, the Wesleys, and the Great Awakening in England changed the face of the nation. William Wilberforce, who led the battle against the slave trade in England, was eleven years old when Whitefield died. Wilberforce's father had died when he was nine, and Wilberforce went to live for a time with his aunt and uncle, William and Hanna Wilberforce. This couple was good friends with George Whitefield.[29]

This was the evangelical air Wilberforce breathed even before he was converted. And after his conversion, Whitefield's vision of the gospel was the truth and the spiritual dynamic that animated Wilberforce's lifelong battle against the slave trade. This is only one small glimpse of the lasting impact of Whitefield and the awakening he served.

So I do not doubt that Whitefield's contemporary, Henry Venn, was right when he said, "[Whitefield] no sooner opened his mouth as a preacher, than God commanded an extraordinary blessing upon his word."[30] Thus, at one level, the explanation of Whitefield's phenomenal impact was God's exceptional anointing on his life.

HIS NATURAL ORATORICAL GIFTS

But at another level, Whitefield held people in thrall who did not believe a single doctrinal word that he said. In other words, we must come to terms with the natural oratorical gifts that he had. How are we to think about these in relation to his effectiveness? Benjamin Franklin, who loved and admired Whitefield[31]—and totally rejected his theology—said,

> Every accent, every emphasis, every modulation of voice, was so perfectly well turned, and well-placed, that without being interested in the subject, one could not help being pleased with the

---

[28] Stout, *Divine Dramatist*, 126.
[29] John Pollock, *Wilberforce* (London: Constable and Company, 1977), 4–5.
[30] Ryle, *Select Sermons of George Whitefield*, 29.
[31] Franklin's comment in a letter about Whitefield was, "He is a good man and I love him." Stout, *Divine Dramatist*, 233.

discourse: a pleasure of much the same kind with that received from an excellent piece of music.[32]

Virtually everyone agrees with Sarah Edwards when she wrote to her brother about Whitefield's preaching:

> He is a born orator. You have already heard of his deep-toned, yet clear and melodious voice. O it is perfect music to listen to that alone! . . . You remember that David Hume thought it worth going 20 miles to hear him speak; and Garrick [an actor who envied Whitefield's gifts] said, 'He could move men to tears . . . in pronouncing the word Mesopotamia.' . . . It is truly wonderful to see what a spell this preacher often casts over an audience by proclaiming the simplest truths of the Bible.[33]

And then she raised one of the questions that has given rise to this book:

> A prejudiced person, I know, might say that this is all theatrical artifice and display; but not so will anyone think who has seen and known him. He is a very devout and godly man, and his only aim seems to be to reach and influence men the best way. He speaks from the heart all aglow with love, and pours out a torrent of eloquence which is almost irresistible.[34]

How does Whitefield's poetic effort—his God-given oratorical abilities—relate to the supernatural effect that we believe he had?

EDWARDS'S MISGIVINGS ABOUT WHITEFIELD'S ORATORY

The story of Jonathan and Sarah Edwards's sincere appreciation for Whitefield is well known. Less known is Edwards's cautions to his people concerning their enthusiasm for Whitefield in the months that followed. I mention this because Edwards's mixed feelings about Whitefield's ministry are part of the issue we are wrestling with—the intersection of the divine and the human in his oratory—his poetic effort.

Whitefield arrived in Northampton on October 17, 1740, stayed

---

[32] Ibid., 204.
[33] Haykin, *Revived Puritan*, 35–37.
[34] Ibid.

four days, and preached four times in Edwards's meeting house. Edwards's wife Sarah commented, "It is wonderful to see what a spell he casts over an audience. . . . I have seen upwards of a thousand people hang on his words with breathless silence, broken only by an occasional half-suppressed sob."[35] When Whitefield was gone, Edwards observed, "The minds of the people in general appeared more engaged in religion, shewing a greater forwardness to make religion the subject of their conversation . . . and to embrace all opportunities to hear the Word preached."[36] Five years had gone by since the fading of the first phase of the Great Awakening in Edwards's parish. Now things were stirring again. And Whitefield seemed to be the decisive instrument.

Nevertheless, Edwards was cautious of uncritical approval and took opportunity to confront Whitefield, gently it seems, concerning several matters such as Whitefield's being guided by "impulses" and Whitefield's too easy judgment of some ministers as unconverted. This dampened the relationship. Edwards says in a letter from 1744, "It is also true (though I don't know that ever I spake of it before) that I thought Mr. Whitefield liked me not so well, for my opposing these things: and though he treated me with great kindness, yet he never made so much of an intimate of me, as of some others."[37]

We can hear echoes of Edwards's concerns in a series of nine sermons he preached the month after Whitefield had left, a series on the parable of the sower from Matthew 13:3–8. He did not name Whitefield, so far as we know, but the cautions he gives shows that he was wrestling with the very poetic effort we are dealing with in its relation to God's supernatural work in the preacher and the hearer.

For example, he says in these messages that people may experience joy when "exceedingly taken with the eloquence of the preacher" and when "pleased with the aptness of expression, and with the fervency, and liveliness, and beautiful gestures of the preacher." But affections grounded in superficial characteristics such as these are not gracious.[38]

---

[35] Quoted in Ava Chamberlain, "The Grand Sower of the Seed: Jonathan Edwards's Critique of George Whitefield," *The New England Quarterly* 70, no. 3 (September 1997), 368.
[36] Ibid., 369.
[37] Quoted in George S. Claghorn, ed., *Letters and Personal Writings: The Works of Jonathan Edwards*, (New Haven, CT: Yale University Press, 1998), 16:157.
[38] Chamberlain, "Grand Sower of the Seed," 378.

Whitefield testified to Edwards's tears as he listened to Whitefield preach. But Edwards cautioned later that "men may shed a great many tears and yet be wholly ignorant of this inward, refreshing, life-giving savor" that is the true foundation for genuine religious affections. If not followed by a "lasting alteration in the frame of the heart," Edwards says the tears may be simply "hypocritical."[39]

Still speaking without naming Whitefield, Edwards warns the people about "talking much of the man, and setting forth the excellency of his manner of delivery, his fervency, affections, and the like." And he remarks that some of his parishioners are "almost ready to follow the preacher to the ends of the earth."[40]

None of these warnings halted the emergence of another phase of the Great Awakening, nor did Edwards intend for them to. Rather, they had the effect he hoped for.

> There are indications that the Northampton revival did take place on Edwards's, and not on Whitefield's, terms. By his own assessment, Edwards was able to avoid the mistakes that, out of ignorance, he had failed to forestall during the earlier awakening. During "the years 1740 and 1741," he reported, "the work seemed to be much more pure, having less of a corrupt mixture, than in the former great outpouring of the Spirit in 1735 and 1736."[41]

Harry Stout, professor of history at Yale, is not optimistic about the purity of Whitefield's motives or the likelihood that his effects were decisively supernatural. He leans toward the judgment of the contemporary of Whitefield, Alexander Garden of South Carolina, who believed that Whitefield "would equally have produced the same Effects, whether he had acted his Part in the Pulpit or on the Stage. . . . It was not the Matter but the Manner, not the Doctrines he delivered, but the Agreeableness of the Delivery," that explained the unprecedented crowds that flocked to hear him preach.[42] Stout's biography, *The Divine Dramatist: George Whitfield and the Rise of Modern Evangelicalism*, is the most sustained piece of historical cynicism I have ever read.

---

[39] Ibid., 379.
[40] Ibid., 380.
[41] Ibid., 382.
[42] Ibid., 384.

THE CONSUMMATE ACTOR?

But the challenge does need to be faced. And I think if we face it head on, what we find is something deeper than what Stout finds. Stout contends that Whitefield never left behind his love for acting and his skill as an actor that was prominent in his youth before his conversion. Thus he says the key to understanding him is "the amalgam of preaching and acting."[43] Whitefield was "the consummate actor."[44] "The fame he sought was . . . the actor's command performance on center stage."[45] "Whitefield was not content simply to talk about the New Birth; he had to sell it with all the dramatic artifice of a huckster."[46] "Tears became Whitefield's . . . psychological gesture."[47] "Whitefield became an actor-preacher, as opposed to a scholar-preacher."[48]

And, of course, this last statement is true, in one sense. He was an actor-preacher as opposed to a scholar-preacher. He was not a Jonathan Edwards. He preached totally without notes,[49] and his traveling pulpit was more of a tiny stage than it was a traditional pulpit.[50] Unlike most of the preachers in his day, he was full of physical action when he preached. Cornelius Winter, Whitefield's young assistant in later years, said,

> I hardly ever knew him go through a sermon without weeping . . . sometimes he exceedingly wept, stamped loudly and passionately, and was frequently so overcome, that, for a few seconds, you would suspect he never could recover; and when he did, nature required some little time to compose himself.[51]

And another contemporary from Scotland, John Gillies, reported how Whitefield moved with "such vehemence upon his bodily frame" that

---

[43] Stout, *Divine Dramatist*, xviii.
[44] Ibid., 42.
[45] Ibid., xxi.
[46] Ibid., 40.
[47] Ibid., 41.
[48] Ibid., xix.
[49] Dallimore, *George Whitefield*, 2:225.
[50] See a picture in Dallimore, *George Whitefield*, between pages 2:303–4, and see a picture of an example of his preaching in Haykin, *Revived Puritan*, 96.
[51] Stout, *Divine Dramatist*, 41. Cornelius Winter also said, "My intimate knowledge of him admits of my acquitting him of the charge of affectation." Eric Carlsson, review of *The Divine Dramatist: George Whitefield and the Rise of Modern Evangelicalism*, by Harry S. Stout, *TrinJ* 14 no. 2 (Fall 1993): 241.

his audience actually shared his exhaustion and "felt a momentary apprehension even for his life."[52]

Therefore, in one sense, I do not doubt that Whitefield was "acting" as he preached. That is, that he was taking the part of the characters in the drama of his sermons and pouring all his energy—his poetic effort—into making their parts real. As when he takes the part of Adam in the Garden and, with a bold and near-blasphemous statement, says to God, "If thou hadst not given me this woman, I had not sinned against thee, so thou mayest thank thyself for my transgression."[53]

WHY WAS HE ACTING?

But the question is: *Why was Whitefield "acting"?* Why was he so full of action and drama? Was he, as Stout claims, "plying a religious trade"?[54] Pursuing "spiritual fame"?[55] Craving "respect and power"?[56] Driven by "egotism"?[57] Putting on "performances"[58] and "integrating religious discourse into the emerging language of consumption"?[59]

I think the most penetrating answer comes from something Whitefield himself said about acting in a sermon in London. In fact, I think it's a key to understanding the power of *his* preaching—and all preaching. James Lockington was present at this sermon and recorded this verbatim. Whitefield is speaking.

> "I'll tell you a story. The Archbishop of Canterbury in the year 1675 was acquainted with Mr. Butterton the [actor]. One day the Archbishop . . . said to Butterton . . . 'Pray inform me Mr. Butterton, what is the reason you actors on stage can affect your congregations with speaking of things imaginary, as if they were real, while we in church speak of things real, which our congregations only receive as if they were imaginary?' 'Why my Lord,' says Butterton, 'the reason is very plain. We actors on stage speak of things imaginary,

---

[52] Stout, *Divine Dramatist*, 141.
[53] Ryle, *Select Sermons of George Whitefield*, 165. The sermon is "Walking with God."
[54] Stout, *Divine Dramatist*, xvii.
[55] Ibid., 21.
[56] Ibid., 36.
[57] Ibid., 55.
[58] Ibid., 71.
[59] Ibid., xviii.

as if they were real and you in the pulpit speak of things real as if they were imaginary.'"

"Therefore," added Whitefield, 'I will bawl [shout loudly], I will not be a velvet-mouthed preacher."[60]

This means that there are three ways to speak. First, you can speak of an unreal, imaginary world as if it were real—that is what actors do in a play. Second, you can speak about a real world as if it were unreal—that is what half-hearted pastors do when they preach about glorious things in a way that implies they are not as terrifying or as wonderful as they are. And third, you can speak about a real spiritual world as if it were wonderfully, terrifyingly, magnificently real, because it is.

OUT-ACTING THE ACTORS

So if you ask Whitefield, "Why do you preach the way you do?" he would probably say, "I believe what I read in the Bible is real." So let me venture this claim: *George Whitefield is not a repressed actor, driven by egotistical love of attention. Rather, he is consciously committed to out-acting the actors because he has seen what is ultimately real.* His oratorical exertion—his poetic effort—is not in *place* of God's revelation and power but in the *service* of them. It is not an expression of ego but of love—for God and for the lost. It is not an effort to get a hearing at any cost but to pay a cost suitable to the beauty and worth of the truth.

He is acting with all his might not because it takes greater gimmicks and charades to convince people of the unreal, but because he had seen something more real than actors on the London stage had ever known. In the very acting, the very speaking, he was seeing, experiencing, the reality of which he spoke. The poetic effort to speak and act in suitable ways wakened in him the reality he wanted to communicate. For him the truths of the gospel were so real—so wonderfully, terrifyingly, magnificently real—that he could not and would not preach them as though they were unreal or merely interesting. He would not treat the greatest facts in the universe as unworthy of his greatest efforts to speak with fitting skill and force.

---

[60] Ibid., 239–40.

ACTING IN THE SERVICE OF REALITY

This was not a repressed acting. This was a released acting. It was not acting in the service of imagination. It was imaginative acting in the service of reality. This was not rendering the imaginary as real. It was rendering the realness of the real as awesomely, breathtakingly real. This was not affectation. This was a passionate re-presentation—replication—of reality. This was not the mighty microscope using all its powers to make the small look impressively big. This was the desperately inadequate telescope turning every power to give some small sense of the majesty of what too many preachers saw as tiresome and unreal.

I don't deny that God uses *natural* vessels to display his *supernatural* reality. And no one denies that George Whitefield was a stupendous natural vessel. He was driven, affable, eloquent, intelligent, empathetic, single minded, steel willed, venturesome, and had a voice like a trumpet that could be heard by thousands outdoors—and sometimes at a distance of two miles. All of these, I venture to say, would have been part of Whitefield's natural gifting even if he had never been born again.

WHITEFIELD BORN AGAIN

But something happened to Whitefield that made all these natural gifts subordinate to another reality. It made them all come into the service of another reality—the glory of Christ in the salvation of sinners. It was the spring of 1735. He was twenty years old. He was part of the Holy Club at Oxford with John and Charles Wesley, and the pursuit of God was all discipline.

> I always chose the worst sort of food. . . . I fasted twice a week. My apparel was mean. . . . I wore woolen gloves, a patched gown, and dirty shoes. . . . I constantly walked out in the cold mornings till part of one of my hands was quite black. . . . I could scarce creep upstairs, I was obliged to inform my kind tutor . . . who immediately sent for a physician to me.[61]

---

[61] Ibid., 25–26.

He took a break from school, and there came into his hands a copy of Henry Scougal's *Life of God in the Soul of Man*. Here is what happened, in his own words:

> I must bear testimony to my old friend Mr. Charles Wesley, he put a book into my hands, called, *The Life of God and the soul of man*, whereby God showed me, that I must be born again, or be damned. I know the place: it may be superstitious, perhaps, but whenever I go to Oxford, I cannot help running to that place where Jesus Christ first revealed himself to me, and gave me the new birth. [Scougal] says, a man may go to church, say his prayers, receive the sacrament, and yet, my brethren, not be a Christian. How did my heart rise, how did my heart shutter, like a poor man that is afraid to look into his account-books, lest he should find himself a bankrupt: yet shall I burn that book, shall I throw it down, shall I put it by, or shall I search into it? I did, and, holding the book in my hand, thus addressed the God of heaven and earth: Lord, if I am not a Christian, if I am not a real one, for Jesus Christ's sake, show me what Christianity is, that I may not be damned at last. I read a little further, and the cheat was discovered; oh, says the author, they that know anything of religion know it is a vital union with the son of God, Christ formed in the heart; oh what a way of divine life did break in upon my poor soul. . . . Oh! With what joy—Joy unspeakable—even joy that was full of, and big with glory, was my soul filled.[62]

The power and depth and the supernatural reality of that change in Whitefield is something Harry Stout—and others who reduce the man to his natural abilities—does not sufficiently reckon with. What happened there was that Whitefield was given the supernatural ability to see what was real. His mind was opened to new reality. Here is the way he described it.

> Above all, my mind being now more opened and enlarged, I began to read the holy Scriptures upon my knees, laying aside all other books, and praying over, if possible, every line and word. This proved meat indeed and drink indeed to my soul. I daily received fresh life, light, and power from above. I got more true knowledge

---

[62] Haykin, *Revived Puritan*, 25–26. From a sermon in 1769.

from reading the book of God in one month than I could ever have acquired from all the writings of men.[63]

This means that Whitefield's acting—his passionate, energetic, whole-souled preaching—was the fruit his new birth because his new birth gave him eyes to see "life and light and power from above." He saw the glorious facts of the gospel as real. Wonderfully, terrifyingly, magnificently real. This is why he cries out, "I will not be a velvet-mouthed preacher."

None of his natural abilities vanished. They were all taken captive to obey Christ (2 Corinthians 10:5). "Let my name be forgotten, let me be trodden under the feet of all men, if Jesus may thereby be glorified."[64]

FIGHTING PRIDE, CONFESSING FOOLISHNESS

Of course he fought pride. Who doesn't fight pride—pride because we *are* somebody, or pride because we *want* to be somebody? But what the record shows is that he fought this fight valiantly, putting to death again and again the vanity of human praise. "It is difficult," he said, "to go through the fiery trial of popularity and applause untainted."[65]

"Commendations," he wrote to a friend, "or even the hinting at them, are poison to a mind addicted to pride. A nail never sinks deeper than when dipt in oil. . . . Pray for me, dear Sir, and heal the wounds you have made. To God alone give glory. To sinners nothing belongs, but shame and confusion."[66]

He confessed publicly the foolishness and mistakes of his earlier years.[67] He confessed to a friend in 1741, "Our most holy thoughts are tinctured with sin, and want the atonement of the Mediator."[68] He cast himself on the free grace that he preached so powerfully:

> I am nothing, have nothing, and can do nothing without God. What although I may, like a polished sepulcher appear a little beautiful without, yet within I am full of pride, self-love and all manner of corruption. However, by the grace of God I am what I am, and if it

---

[63] Ryle, *Select Sermons of George Whitefield*, 15.
[64] Carlsson, review of *Divine Dramatist*: 244.
[65] Haykin, *Revived Puritan*, 68.
[66] Ibid., 83.
[67] Dallimore, *George Whitefield*, 2:168, 241.
[68] Haykin, *Revived Puritan*, 50.

should please God to make me instrumental to do the least good, not unto me, but unto him, be all the glory.[69]

MAKING REAL THINGS REAL

So Whitefield had a new nature. He had been born again. And this new nature enabled him to see what was real. And Whitefield knew in his soul: *I will never speak of what is real as though it is imaginary. I will not be a velvet-mouthed preacher.* He would not abandon acting. He would out-act the actors in his preaching, because they became actors to make imaginary things look real, and he became the preacher-actor to make real things look like what they are. This was Herbert's passion with his crafted poetry and Whitefield's passion with his dramatic preaching. They both sought to use words—crafted words, heralded words—in such a way as to waken the reader and the listener to things that no mere words could communicate.

Whitefield didn't pause in his preaching to have a little drama off to the side—like some preachers do today, a little skit, a little clip from a movie—that would have missed the whole point. Preaching *was* the play. Preaching *was* the drama. The reality of the gospel had consumed *him*. That *was* the witness. The preaching itself had become the active word of God. God was speaking. Reality was not simply being shown. Reality was happening in the preaching.

NOT ACTING IN THE THEATRICAL SENSE

What this means is that in the end, Whitefield's "acting" was not acting in the theatrical sense at all. If a woman has a role in a movie, say, the mother of child caught in a burning house, and as the cameras are focused on her, she is screaming to the firemen and pointing to the window in the second floor, we all say she is acting. But if a house is on fire in your neighborhood, and you see a mother screaming to the firemen and pointing to the window in the second floor, nobody says she's acting. Why not? They look exactly the same.

It's because there really is a child up there in the fire. This woman really is the child's mother. There is real danger that the child could

---

[69] Ibid., 103.

die. Everything is real. And that's the way it was for Whitefield. The new birth had opened his eyes to what was real and to the magnitude of what was real: God, creation, humanity, sin, Satan, divine justice and wrath, heaven, hell, incarnation, the perfections of Christ, his death, atonement, redemption, propitiation, resurrection, the Holy Spirit, saving grace, forgiveness, justification, reconciliation with God, peace, sanctification, love, the second coming of Christ, the new heaven and the new earth, and everlasting joy. These were real. Overwhelmingly real to him. And infinitely important. He had been born again. He had eyes to see.

When he warned of wrath, pleaded for people to escape, and lifted up Christ, he wasn't playacting. He was calling down the kind of emotions and actions that correspond with such realities. That's what preaching does. It seeks to exalt Christ, and describe sin, and offer salvation, and persuade sinners with words and actions and emotions that correspond to the weight of these realities. George Herbert stuns us again and again with new glimpses of Christ in his startling turns of phrase, his unexpected endings that do anything but end our vision. Whitefield stunned his audiences with the glimpses of Christ in his dramatic reenactments of the greatest realities in the world.

If you see these realities with the eyes of your heart, and if you feel the weight of them, you will know that such poetry is not pretense and such preaching is not playacting. The house is burning. There are people trapped on the second floor. We love them. And there is a way of escape.

THE PRECIOUSNESS OF "THE DOCTRINES OF GRACE"

Let's be more specific. What did George Whitefield see as real? Unlike so much preaching today, the preaching of the eighteenth-century awakening—including the evangelistic preaching of Whitefield and Wesley—was doctrinally specific and not vague. When you read the sermons of Whitefield, you are struck with how amazingly doctrinal they are.

What Whitefield saw within months after his conversion, just as George Herbert saw so differently than John Donne, was the precious-

ness and power of the "doctrines of grace."[70] What was real for him
was classical evangelical Calvinism. "From first to last," Stout says, "he
was a Calvinist who believed that God chose him for salvation and not
the reverse."[71] J. I. Packer observes that "Whitefield was entirely free
of doctrinal novelties."[72]

EMBRACING THE CALVINISTIC SCHEME

His guide as he read the Bible in those formative days was not John Calvin but Matthew Henry.[73] "I embrace the Calvinistic scheme," he said,
"not because Calvin, but Jesus Christ has taught it to me."[74] In fact, he
wrote to John Wesley in 1740, "I never read anything that Calvin wrote."[75]

He believed these biblical truths—which he sometimes called "the
doctrines of the Reformation"—did the most to "debase man and exalt
the Lord Jesus. . . . All others leave free will in man, and make him, in
part at least, a Savior to himself."[76] And not only did that diminish the
work of the Savior, it made our position in Christ insecure.

THE LINK BETWEEN ELECTION AND PERSEVERANCE

What Whitefield saw as real with his new eyes was the link between
election and perseverance. God had chosen him unconditionally, and
God would therefore keep him invincibly. This was his rock-solid
confidence and a fire in his bones and the power of his obedience. He
wrote in 1739 from Philadelphia,

> Oh the excellency of the doctrine of election, and of the saints' final
> perseverance, to those who are truly sealed by the Spirit of promise!
> I am persuaded, till a man comes to believe and feel these impor-
> tant truths, he cannot come out of himself; but when convinced of

---

[70] He used the term freely for the fullness of the Reformation and Calvinistic teaching about salvation
by sovereign grace. Writing on February 20, 1741, to Anne Dutton, he refers to his settlement in Georgia
and says, "My family in Georgia was once sadly shaken, but now, blessed be God, it is settled, and, I
hope, established in the doctrines of grace." Ibid., 127. On his second trip to America, he was critical
of many pastors, saying, "Many ministers are so sadly degenerated from their pious ancestors, that the
doctrines of grace, especially the personal, all-sufficient righteousness of Jesus is but too seldom, too
slightly mentioned." Stout, *Divine Dramatist*, 97.
[71] Stout, *Divine Dramatist*, xxiii.
[72] Packer, "Spirit with the Word," 56.
[73] Haykin, *Revived Puritan*, 26.
[74] Packer, " Spirit with the Word," 47.
[75] Dallimore, *George Whitefield*,1:574.
[76] Haykin, *Revived Puritan*, 76.

these, and assured of the application of them to his own heart, he then walks by faith indeed, not in himself but in the Son of God, who died and gave himself for him. Love, not fear, constrains him to obedience.[77]

And a year later he wrote to John Wesley, "The doctrine of election, and the final perseverance of those that are truly in Christ, I am ten thousand times more convinced of, if possible, then when I saw you last."[78] He loved the assurance he had in the mighty hands of God. "Surely I am safe, because put into his almighty arms. Though I may fall, yet I shall not utterly be cast away. The Spirit of the Lord Jesus will hold, and uphold me."[79]

TELLING THE GOSPEL WITH ALL HIS MIGHT

And he didn't just quietly enjoy these realities for himself. George Whitefield and George Herbert had seen the beauties of God's grace and the horrors of sin, and neither could leave these things unexpressed. Neither would keep them to himself. Herbert hoped his work would bless many, but he left it to his friend Nicholas Ferrar to render that judgment. Just before he died he sent his life's work of unpublished poems through a common acquaintance with the words: "If [Nicholas] can think it may turn to the advantage of any dejected poor soul, let it be made public; if not, let him burn it; for I and it are less than the least of God's mercies."[80]

Similarly, Whitefield would not keep his passion for the glories of Christ and the doctrines of grace to himself. They were woven into all his evangelistic messages.

He said to Wesley, "I must preach the Gospel of Christ, and this I cannot now do without speaking of election."[81] In his sermon based on 1 Corinthians 1:30 called "Christ the Believer's Wisdom, Righteousness, Sanctification, and Redemption," he exults in the doctrine (remember he is lifting up his voice to thousands):

---

[77] Ibid., 71–72.
[78] Ibid., 113.
[79] Ibid., 76.
[80] Quotation from Izaak Walton's *The Life of Mr. George Herbert* (1670), quoted in John Tobin, ed., *George Herbert: The Complete English Poems* (New York: Penguin, 1991), 310–11.
[81] Dallimore, *George Whitefield*, 2:41.

For my part I cannot see how true humbleness of mind can be attained without a knowledge of [the doctrine of election]; and though I will not say, that every one who denies election is a bad man, yet I will say, with that sweet singer, Mr. Trail, it is a very bad sign: such a one, whoever he be, I think cannot truly know himself; for, if we deny election, we must, partly at least, glory in ourselves; but our redemption is so ordered, that no flesh should glory in the Divine presence; and hence it is, that the pride of man opposes this doctrine, because, according to this doctrine, and no other, "he that glories must glory only in the Lord."

But what shall I say? Election is a mystery that shines with such resplendent brightness, that, to make use of the words of one who has drunk deeply of electing love, it dazzles the weak eyes even of some of God's children; however, though they know it not, all the blessing they receive, all the privileges they do or will enjoy, through Jesus Christ, flow from the everlasting love of God the Father.[82]

OFFERING JESUS FREELY TO EVERY SOUL

And Whitefield reminds Wesley—and us—in a letter of 1741, "Though I hold particular election, yet I offer Jesus freely to every individual soul."[83] Indeed, Whitefield does not hide his understanding of the Calvinistic doctrines of definite atonement or irresistible grace as he pleads with men to come to Christ. In a sermon on John 10:27–28 called "The Good Shepherd," he speaks clearly of the particular sense in which Christ died for his own,

If you belong to Jesus Christ, he is speaking of you; for says he, "I know my sheep." "I know them"; what does that mean? Why, he knows their number, he knows their names, he knows every one for whom he died; and if there were to be one missing for whom Christ died, God the Father would send him down again from heaven to fetch him.[84]

And then he mounts his passionate plea on the basis of irresistible sovereign grace:

---

[82] Haykin, *Revived Puritan*, 97–98.
[83] Ibid.,145.
[84] Ryle, *Select Sermons of George Whitefield*, 193.

O come, come, see what it is to have eternal life; do not refuse it; haste, sinner, haste away: may the great, the good Shepherd, draw your souls. Oh! If you never heard his voice before, God grant you may hear it now. . . . O come! Come! Come to the Lord Jesus Christ; to him I leave you. . . . Amen.[85]

THE PROMINENCE OF JUSTIFICATION

Among the doctrines of the Reformation that filled his great evangelistic sermons, the most prominent was the doctrine of justification. His signature sermon, if there was one, seemed to be "The Lord Our Righteousness" based on Jeremiah 23:6. He never elevated justification to the exclusion of regeneration and sanctification. In fact, he was explicit in his effort to keep them in balance:

> We must not put asunder what God has joined together; we must keep the medium between the two extremes; not insist so much on the one hand upon Christ without, as to exclude Christ within, as evidence of our being his, and as a preparation for future happiness; nor on the other hand, so depend on inherent righteousness or holiness wrought in us, as to exclude the righteousness of Jesus Christ without us.[86]

THE GLORY OF JESUS'S OBEDIENCE IMPUTED

But O how jealous he is again and again to press home to the masses the particularities of this doctrine, especially the imputation of Christ's obedience. He lamented in one sermon,

> I fear they understand justification in that low sense, which I understood it in a few years ago, as implying no more than remission of sins; but it not only signifies remission of sins past, but also a *federal right* to all good things to come. . . . As the obedience of Christ is imputed to believers so his perseverance in that obedience is to be imputed to them also.[87]

---

[85] Ibid., 199. Also see page 112 for another illustration of how he pleads with people even while drawing their attention to the fact that they cannot change themselves.
[86] Ibid., 106.
[87] Ibid., 107.

> Never did greater or more absurdities flow from the denying any doctrine, than will flow from denying the doctrine of Christ's imputed righteousness.[88]

> The world says, because we preach faith we deny good works; this is the usual objection against the doctrine of imputed righteousness. But it is a slander, an impudent slander.[89]

RELENTLESSLY DEVOTED TO GOOD DEEDS

And, indeed, it was a slander in the life of George Whitefield. Whitefield was relentless in his devotion to good deeds and his care for the poor—constantly raising funds for orphans and other mercy ministries.[90] Benjamin Franklin, who enjoyed one of the warmest friendships Whitefield ever had, in spite of their huge religious differences, said, "[Whitefield's] integrity, disinterestedness and indefatigable zeal in prosecuting every good work, I have never seen equaled, I shall never see excelled."[91]

In other words, Whitefield's impassioned belief in the imputation of Christ's righteousness did not hinder the practical pursuit of justice and love—it empowered it. This connection between doctrine and practical duties of love was one of the secrets of Whitefield's power. The masses believed, and believed rightly, that he practiced what he preached. The new birth and justification by faith made a person good.

A CONTRADICTORY FIGURE

But it didn't make a person perfect. It didn't make Whitefield perfect. In fact, one of the effects of reading history, and biography in particular, is the persistent discovery of contradictions and paradoxes of sin and righteousness in the holiest people.

Whitefield is no exception and he will be more rightly honored if we are honest about his blindness as well as his doctrinal faithfulness

---

[88] Ibid., 129.
[89] Ibid., 189.
[90] "[Whitefield] was doctrinally pure in his insistence that salvation came only through God's grace, *but* he was nevertheless [sic] deeply involved in charitable work, and his year-long tour through America was to raise money for an orphanage in Georgia. He raised more money than any other cleric of his time for philanthropies, which included schools, libraries, and almshouses across Europe and America." Walter Isaacson, *Benjamin Franklin: An American Life* (New York: Simon & Schuster, 2003), 110.
[91] Carlsson, review of *Divine Dramatist*: 245.

and goodness. The most glaring blindness of his life—and there were others—was his support for the American enslavement of blacks.

SLAVEHOLDER

Before it was legal to own slaves in Georgia, Whitefield advocated for the legalization with a view to making the orphanage he built more affordable.[92] In 1748, he wrote to the trustees of Bethesda, the name of his orphanage and settlement,

> Had a Negro been allowed, I should now have had a sufficiency to support a great many orphans, without expending about half the sum which hath been laid out. . . . Georgia never can or will be a flourishing province without negroes [sic] are allowed. . . . I am as willing as ever to do all I can for *Georgia* and the orphan house, if either a limited use of negroes is approved of, or some more indentured servants sent over. If not, I cannot promise to keep any large family, or cultivate the plantation in any consider-able manner.[93]

In 1752, Georgia became a royal colony. Slavery was legalized, and Whitefield joined the ranks of the slave owners that he had denounced in his earlier years.[94]

ARDENT SLAVE EVANGELIST

That, in itself, was not unusual. Most of the slaveholders were profess-ing Christians. But in Whitefield's case things were more complex. He didn't fit the mold of wealthy, Southern plantation owner. Almost all of them resisted evangelizing and educating the slaves. They knew intuitively that education would tend toward equality, which would undermine the whole system. And evangelism would imply that slaves could become children of God, which would mean that they were brothers and sisters to the owners, which would also undermine the

---

[92] "Whitefield spent much of his time in the South actively promoting the legalization of slavery in Georgia." Stout, *Divine Dramatist*, 198.

[93] Ibid., 199.

[94] "There was no longer a need for the South Carolina plantation. All resources were transferred to Bethesda, including a force of slaves for whom, Whitefield rejoiced, 'Nothing seems to be wanted but a good overseer, to instruct the negroes in selling and planting.'" Ibid., 218.

whole system. That's why the apparent New Testament tolerance of slavery is in fact a very powerful subversion of the institution.

Ironically, Whitefield did more to bring Christianity to the slave community in Georgia than anyone else.[95] Whitefield wrote letters to newspapers defending the evangelism of slaves and arguing that to deny them this was to deny that they had souls (which many did deny). Harry Stout observes, "In fact, the letters represented the first journalistic statement on the subject of slavery. As such, they marked a precedent of awesome implications, beyond anything Whitefield could have imagined."[96]

Whitefield said he was willing to face the "whip" of Southern planters if they disapproved of his preaching the new birth to the slaves.[97] He recounts one of his customary efforts among the slaves in North Carolina on his second trip to America:

> I went, as my usual custom . . . among the negroes belonging to the house. One man was sick in bed, and two of his children said their prayers after me very well. This more and more convinces me that negro children, if early brought up in the nurture and admonition of the Lord, would make as great proficiency as any among white people's children. I do not despair, if God spares my life, of seeing a school of young negroes singing the praises of Him Who made them, in a psalm of thanksgiving. Lord, Thou has put into my heart a good design to educate them; I doubt not but Thou wilt enable me to bring it to good effect.[98]

Gary B. Nash dates "the advent of black Christianity" in Philadelphia to Whitefield's first preaching tour. He estimates that perhaps one thousand slaves heard Whitefield's sermons in Philadelphia. What they heard was that they had souls just as surely as the white people. Whitefield's work for the slaves in Philadelphia was so effective that Philadelphia's most prominent dancing master, Robert Bolton, renounced his old vocation and turned his school over to blacks. "By summer's end, over 50 'black Scholars' had arrived at the school."[99]

---

[95] Ibid., 101.
[96] Ibid., 123.
[97] Ibid., 100.
[98] Ibid., 101.
[99] Ibid., 107–8.

Sowing the Seeds of Equality

From Georgia to North Carolina to Philadelphia, Whitefield sowed the seeds of equality through heartfelt evangelism and education—blind as he was, it seems, to the contradiction of this equality with buying and selling slaves.

Whitefield ended his most famous sermon, "The Lord Our Righteousness" with this appeal to the blacks in the crowd:

> Here, then, I conclude; but I must not forget the *poor negroes*: no, I must not. Jesus Christ has died for them, as well as for others. Nor do I mention you last, because I despise your souls, but because I would have what I shall say make the deeper impression upon your hearts. O that you would seek the Lord to be your righteousness! Who knows but he may be found of you? For in Jesus Christ there is neither male nor female, bond nor free; even you may be the children of God, if you believe in Jesus. . . . Christ Jesus is the same now as he was yesterday, and will wash you in his own blood. Go home then, turn the word of the text into a prayer, and entreat the Lord to be your righteousness. Even so. Come Lord Jesus, come quickly in all our souls. *Amen*. Lord Jesus, *amen*, and *amen*!

This kind of preaching infuriated many slave owners. One wonders if there was a rumbling in Whitefield's own soul because he really did perceive where such radical evangelism would lead. He went public with his censures of slave owners and published words like these: "God has a quarrel with you" for treating slaves "as though they were Brutes." If these slaves were to rise up in rebellion, "all good Men must acknowledge the judgment would be just."[100]

This was incendiary. But it was too early in the course of history. Apparently Whitefield did not perceive fully the implications of what he was saying. What was clear was that the slave population loved Whitefield. For all his imperfections and blindness to the contradiction between advocating slavery and undermining slavery, when he died, it was the blacks who expressed the greatest grief in America.[101] More than any other eighteenth-century figure, Whitefield established

---

[100] Ibid., 101–2.
[101] Ibid., 284.

Christian faith in the slave community. Whatever else he failed in, for this service they were deeply thankful.

A seventeen-year-old black Boston servant girl named Phillis Wheatley (1753–1784) wrote one of his most famous elegies. Wheatley would become one of the best known poets in pre-nineteenth-century America.

> Pampered in the household of prominent Boston commercialist John Wheatley, lionized in New England and England, with presses in both places publishing her poems, and paraded before the new republic's political leadership and the old empire's aristocracy, Phillis was the abolitionists' illustrative testimony that blacks could be both artistic and intellectual. Her name was a household word among literate colonists and her achievements a catalyst for the fledgling antislavery movement.[102]

It was the Whitefield elegy that brought Wheatley national renown. "Published as a broadside and a pamphlet in Boston, Newport, and Philadelphia, the poem was published with Ebenezer Pemberton's funeral sermon for Whitefield in London in 1771, bringing her international acclaim."[103] In it she paid her due in tribute to Whitefield's love for "Africans."

> He offer'd THAT he did himself receive,
> A greater gift not GOD himself can give:
> He urg'd the need of HIM to every one;
> It was no less than GOD's co-equal SON!
>
> . . . .
>
> Take HIM ye *Africans*, he longs for you;
> Impartial SAVIOUR, is his title due;
> If you will choose to walk in grace's road,
> You shall be sons, and kings, and priests to GOD.[104]

---

[102] "Phillis Wheatley," *Poetry Foundation*, accessed August 2, 2013, http://www.poetryfoundation.org/bio/phillis-wheatley.
[103] Ibid.
[104] Phillis Wheatley, "An Elegiac Poem on the Death of That Celebrated Divine, and Eminent Servant of Jesus Christ, the Late Reverend, and Pious George Whitefield," (1771), *A Celebration of Women Writers*, ed. Mary Mark Ockerbloom, accessed January 13, 2014, www.digital.library.upenn.edu/women/wheatley/whitefield/whitefield.html.

Indeed, it is a beautiful providence that Whitefield's spiritual power and poetic eloquence should find their first and (at that time) most influential expression in a poem of a black slave. It is worth reading in full:

AN ELEGIAC POEM, ON THE DEATH OF THAT CELEBRATED DIVINE, AND EMINENT SERVANT OF JESUS CHRIST, THE LATE REVEREND, AND PIOUS GEORGE WHITEFIELD

> Hail, happy Saint, on thine immortal throne!
> To thee complaints of grievance are unknown;
> We hear no more the music of thy tongue,
> Thy wonted auditories cease to throng.
> Thy lessons in unequal'd accents flow'd!
> While emulation in each bosom glow'd;
> Thou didst, in strains of eloquence refin'd,
> Inflame the soul, and captivate the mind.
> Unhappy we, the setting Sun deplore!
> Which once was splendid, but it shines no more;
> He leaves this earth for Heav'n's unmeasur'd height;
> And worlds unknown, receive him from our sight.
> There WHITEFIELD wings, with rapid course his way,
> And sails to Zion, through vast seas of day.
>
> When his AMERICANS were burden'd sore,
> When streets were crimson'd with their guiltless gore!
> Unrival'd friendship in his breast now strove:
> The fruit thereof was charity and love
> Towards *America*—couldst thou do more
> Than leave thy native home, the *British* shore,
> To cross the great Atlantic's wat'ry road,
> To see *America's* distress'd abode?
> Thy prayers, great Saint, and thy incessant cries,
> Have pierc'd the bosom of thy native skies!
> Thou moon hast seen, and ye bright stars of light
> Have witness been of his requests by night!
> He pray'd that grace in every heart might dwell:
> He long'd to see *America* excell;

He charg'd its youth to let the grace divine
Arise, and in their future actions shine;
He offer'd THAT he did himself receive,
A greater gift not GOD himself can give:
He urg'd the need of HIM to every one;
It was no less than GOD's co-equal SON!
Take HIM ye wretched for your only good;
Take HIM ye starving souls to be your food.
Ye thirsty, come to this life giving stream:
Ye Preachers, take him for your joyful theme:
Take HIM, "my dear AMERICANS," he said,
Be your complaints in his kind bosom laid:
Take HIM ye *Africans*, he longs for you;
Impartial SAVIOUR, is his title due;
If you will chuse to walk in grace's road,
You shall be sons, and kings, and priests to GOD.

Great COUNTESS![105] we *Americans* revere
Thy name, and thus condole thy grief sincere:
We mourn with thee, that TOMB obscurely plac'd,
In which thy Chaplain undisturb'd doth rest.
New-England sure, doth feel the ORPHAN's smart;
Reveals the true sensations of his heart:
Since this fair Sun, withdraws his golden rays,
No more to brighten these distressful days!
His lonely *Tabernacle*, sees no more
A WHITEFIELD landing on the *British* shore:
Then let us view him in yon azure skies:
Let every mind with this lov'd object rise.
No more can he exert his lab'ring breath,
Seiz'd by the cruel messenger of death.
What can his dear AMERICA return?
But drop a tear upon his happy urn,
Thou tomb, shalt safe retain thy sacred trust,
Till life divine re-animate his dust.[106]

---

[105] The Countess of Huntington, who gave hearty support to the evangelical awakening in England and for whom Whitefield functioned as a chaplain.
[106] Wheatley, "Elegiac Poem."

A SINNER FIT TO PREACH FREE GRACE

So the greatest preacher of the eighteenth century, perhaps in the history of the Christian church, was a paradoxical figure. There was, as he himself so freely confessed, sin remaining in him. And that is what we have found in every human soul on this earth—except one. Which is why our lives are meant to point to him—that sinless one. Christ's perfect obedience, not ours, is the foundation of our acceptance with God. If then, our sin, as well as our righteousness, can point people away from ourselves to Christ, we will rejoice even as we repent.

"I know no other reason," Whitefield said, "why Jesus has put me into the ministry, than because I am the chief of sinners, and therefore fittest to preach free grace to a world lying in the wicked one."[107] Yes. But as we have seen, God would make not only his unworthiness redound to the grace of God, but also his passionate oratory, his natural dramatic giftedness, and his poetic effort. This too, imperfect as it was, no doubt contaminated as it was with flawed motives, God made the instrument of his supernatural work of salvation. No eloquence can save a soul. But the worth of salvation and the worth of souls impels preachers to speak and write with all their might in ways that say: there is more, there is so much more beauty—so much more glory—for you to see than I can say.

---

[107] Haykin, *Revived Puritan*, 157–58.

Mythologies . . . are products of imagination in the sense that their content is imaginative. The more imaginative ones are "near the mark" in the sense that they communicate more Reality to us.

C. S. Lewis
Personal letter

[The epic of Oedipus] may not be "like real life" in the superficial sense: but it sets before us an image of what reality may well be like at some more central region.

A great romance is like a flower whose smell reminds you of something you can't quite place. . . . I've never met Orcs or Ents or Elves—but the feel of it, the sense of a huge past, of lowering danger, of heroic tasks achieved by the most apparently unheroic people, of distance, vastness, strangeness, homeliness (all blended together) is so exactly what living feels like to me.

C. S. Lewis
"On Stories"

3

C. S. Lewis—Romantic, Rationalist, Likener, Evangelist

How Lewis's Paths to Christ Shaped His Life and Ministry

We begin with an accolade from Peter Kreeft, professor of philosophy at Boston College:

> Once upon a dreary era, when the world of . . . specialization had nearly made obsolete all universal geniuses, romantic poets, Platonic idealists, rhetorical craftsmen, and even orthodox Christians, there appeared a man (almost as if from another world, one of the worlds of his own fiction: was he a man or something more like elf or Angel?) who was all of these things as amateur, as well as probably the world's foremost authority in his professional province, Medieval and Renaissance English literature. Before his death in 1963 he found time to produce some first-quality works of literary history, literary criticism, theology, philosophy, autobiography, biblical studies, historical philology, fantasy, science fiction, letters, poems, sermons, formal and informal essays, a historical novel, a spiritual diary, religious allegory, short stories, and children's novels. Clive Staples Lewis was not a man: he was a world.[1]

---

[1] Peter Kreeft, *C. S. Lewis: A Critical Essay* (Grand Rapids, MI: Eerdmans, 1969), 4.

Those are the kinds of accolades you read again and again. Which means there must have been something extraordinary about the man. Indeed, there was.

Speaking personally, ever since I began to take him and his Reformed counterpart, Jonathan Edwards, seriously in my early twenties, I have never been the same. I don't see myself as an imitator of Lewis and Edwards. The kind of Joy that Lewis and Edwards spoke of cannot be imitated. It's a gift. You don't make it happen. And both these men are intellectual giants in the land. I don't have their intellectual ability. In their ability to see and think and feel, they are almost without peer. Their capacities to see and feel the freshness and wonder of things was childlike, and their capacities to describe it and understand it and defend it was massively manly.

Ruth Pitter was a poet and close friend of Lewis, and described it so well. She said,

> His whole life was oriented and motivated by an almost uniquely-persisting child's sense of glory and of nightmare. The adult events were received into a medium still as pliable as wax, wide open to the glory, and equally vulnerable, with a man's strength to feel it all, and a great scholar's and writer's skills to express and to interpret.[2]

So I can't imitate Lewis, but I can listen. And I have been listening for decades, and what I have heard and seen echoes almost everywhere in my life and work. His influence is simply enormous.

CHILDHOOD, SCHOOLING, AND BECOMING THE VOICE

The focus of this chapter is not mainly on Lewis's biographical details, but we do need an outline of his life to see what kind of life gave birth to his ideas. So here is a short summary of his life—the hard facts, you might say. Lewis loved hard facts. The kind you want under your house when the rains come down and the floods come up.

Lewis was born in 1898 in Belfast, Ireland. His mother died when he was nine years old, and his father never remarried. Between the

---

[2] Ruth Pitter quoted in Alan Jacobs, *The Narnian* (New York: HarperOne, 2005), xxii.

death of his mother in August 1908 and the fall of 1914, Lewis attended four different boarding schools. Then for two and a half years, he studied with William Kirkpatrick, whom he called "the Great Knock." And there his emerging atheism was confirmed, and his reasoning powers were refined in an extraordinary way. Lewis said, "If ever a man came near to being a purely logical entity that man was Kirk."[3] He described himself later as a seventeen-year-old rationalist.

But just as his rationalism was at its peak, he stumbled onto George MacDonald's fantasy novel *Phantastes*. "That night," he said, "my imagination was, in a certain sense, baptized."[4] Something had broken in—a "new quality," a "bright shadow," he called it.[5] The romantic impulse of his childhood was again awake. Only now it seemed real, and holy (though he would not have called it that yet).

At eighteen, he took his place at Oxford University, but before he could begin his studies he entered the army, and in February 1918 was wounded in France and returned to England to recover. He resumed his studies at Oxford in January 1919, and over the next six years took three First Class Honors in classics, humanities, and English literature. He became a teaching fellow in October 1925, at the age of twenty-six.

Six years later in 1931, he professed faith in Jesus Christ and was settled in the conviction that Christianity is true. Within ten years, he had become the "voice of faith" for the nation of England during the Second World War, and his broadcast talks in 1941–1942 "achieved classic status."[6]

LEWIS IN FULL FLOWER

He was now in the full flower of his creative and apologetic productivity. In his prime, he was probably the world's leading authority on Medieval English literature, and according to one of his adversaries, "the best read man of his generation."[7] But he was vastly more. Books of many kinds were rolling out: *Pilgrim's Regress*, *The Allegory of Love*, *Screwtape Letters*, and *Perelandra*. Then in 1950, he began the Chronicles

---

[3] C. S. Lewis, *Surprised by Joy* (New York: Harcourt, Brace, & World, 1955), 135.
[4] Ibid., 181.
[5] Ibid., 179.
[6] Alister McGrath, *C. S. Lewis—A Life: Eccentric Genius, Reluctant Prophet* (Carol Stream, IL: Tyndale, 2013), 210.
[7] Ibid., 166.

of Narnia. All these titles were of different genres and showed the amazing versatility of Lewis as a writer and thinker and imaginative visionary.

He appeared on the cover of *Time Magazine* in 1947. Then, after thirty years at Oxford, he took a professorship in Medieval and Renaissance English at the University of Cambridge in 1955. The next year, at the age of fifty-seven, he married Joy Davidman. And just short of their fourth anniversary, she died of cancer. Three and a half years later—two weeks short of his sixty-fifth birthday, on November 22, 1963—Lewis followed her in death.

Lewis as an author is more popular today than at any time during his life. The Chronicles of Narnia alone have gone on to sell over one hundred million copies in forty languages.[8] One of the reasons for this appeal, I will argue, is that Lewis is a "romantic rationalist" to an exceptionally high and healthy degree. His poetic effort and his rational effort combined in a kind of writing and speaking that was exceptionally illuminating on almost everything he touched.

Lewis's Defective Views

Before I unfold what that means, it's important to confess that, for all the accolades, Lewis is not exemplary in all his views. Some readers may see quickly the common denominator between George Herbert and George Whitefield, on the one hand, and C. S. Lewis, on the other—namely, the conviction and demonstration that poetic effort is a path to seeing more truth and more beauty. That is what we have seen in the experience of Herbert and Whitefield. Now Lewis says, it is often the case that highly imaginative stories "are 'near the mark' in the sense that *they communicate more Reality to us.*"[9] Ironically, then, the effort to describe reality in creative and wondrous language often takes us deeper into that reality. If you see this common denominator, the inclusion of Herbert and Whitefield and Lewis in one volume will make sense.

But some readers will realize that Lewis was not the kind of his-

---

[8] Jonathan Luxmoore, "C. S. Lewis 'Couldn't Touch Anything without Illuminating It,'" *National Catholic Reporter*, accessed December 18, 2013, http://www.ncronline.org/news/art-media/cs-lewis-couldnt-touch-anything-without-illuminating-it.
[9] Walter Hooper, ed., *The Collected Letters of C. S. Lewis: Books, Broadcasts, and War, 1931–1949*, vol. 2 (San Francisco: HarperCollins, 2007), 445 (emphasis added).

toric, Reformed evangelical Christian that Herbert and Whitefield were. Doctrinally his differences from them, and from me, are significant. We would do him a disservice not to take this into account.

Scripture, Reformation, Catholicism

For example, Lewis doesn't believe in the inerrancy of Scripture. He claims Jesus predicted his second coming within one generation and calls this prediction an "error."[10] He treats the Reformation as an unnecessary intramural fracas and thinks it could have been avoided. He calls aspects of it farcical.[11] He steadfastly refused in public or in letters to explain why he was not a Roman Catholic but remained in the Church of England.

Salvation without Knowing Christ?

He makes room for at least some people to be saved through imperfect representations of Christ in other religions. After visiting Greece with his dying wife, he wrote, "At Daphne it was hard not to pray to Apollo the Healer. But somehow one didn't feel it would have been very wrong—would only have been addressing Christ *sub specie Apollinis*."[12] In this way of talking about possibly praying to Christ through Apollo, he is suggesting something similar to the counsel he gave a mother who feared her son loved Aslan more than Jesus:

> Laurence can't really love Aslan more than Jesus, even if he feels that's what he's doing. For the things he loves Aslan for doing or saying are simply the things Jesus really did and said. So that when Laurence thinks he is loving Aslan, he is really loving Jesus: and perhaps loving him more than he ever did before.[13]

---

[10] C. S. Lewis, "The World's Last Night" in *C. S. Lewis: Essay Collection and Other Short Pieces*, ed. Lesley Walmsley (London: HarperCollins, 2000), 45. See also Michael Christensen's study of Lewis's view of Scripture, *C. S. Lewis on Scripture* (Waco, TX: Word, 1979), 91. And the very helpful essay by Philip Ryken, "Inerrancy and the Patron Saint of Evangelicalism: C. S. Lewis on Holy Scripture," in *The Romantic Rationalist: God, Life, and Imagination in the Work of C. S. Lewis*, ed. John Piper and David Mathis (Wheaton, IL: Crossway, 2014).

[11] "The process whereby 'Faith and Works' became a stock gag in the commercial theater is characteristic of that whole tragic farce which we call the history of the Reformation." C. S. Lewis, *English Literature in the Sixteenth Century: Excluding Drama* (Oxford: Oxford University Press, 1953), 37.

[12] Lewis to Chad Walsh, 23 May 1960, in *Letters of C. S. Lewis*, ed. W. H. Lewis and Walter Hooper, rev. ed. (New York: Harcourt Brace Jovanovich, 1993), 488.

[13] C. S. Lewis to a mother, *Letters to Children*, ed. Lyle W. Dorsett and Marjorie Lamp Mead (New York: Macmillian, 1985), 57.

The most familiar instance of suggesting people can be saved without knowing Jesus is the entrance of Emeth into heaven at the end of *The Last Battle*. Emeth is the Hebrew word of "faithful" or "true" and represents a sincere seeker in a religion that does not know Aslan, at least not by his real name.[14]

The most sweeping statement of this view that some are saved without knowing Christ is found in his answer to a Mrs. Johnson who wrote to him and asked, "What happens to Jews who are still waiting for the Messiah?" Lewis answers:

> I think that every prayer which is sincerely made even to a false god, or to a very imperfectly conceived true God, is accepted by the true God and that Christ saves many who do not think they know Him. For He is (dimly) present in the good side of the inferior teachers they follow. In the parable of the Sheep & Goats (Matt. XXV. 31 and following) those who are saved do not seem to know that they have served Christ. But of course our anxiety about unbelievers is most usefully employed when it leads us not to speculation but to earnest prayer for them and the attempt to be in our own lives such good advertisements for Christianity as will make it attractive.[15]

Free Will and Atonement

On another point, Lewis's case for free will as a way to explain why there is suffering in the world seems to run counter to biblical texts on the sovereignty of God.[16] But we must be careful here because he did not give us a systematic statement of his views, and they do not all point toward a traditional view of free will as ultimate self-determination.[17]

---

[14] C. S. Lewis, *The Last Battle* (New York: Macmillan, 1957), 155–57.

[15] Walter Hooper, ed., *The Collected Letters of C. S. Lewis: Narnia, Cambridge, and Joy, 1950–1963*, vol. 3 (San Francisco: HarperCollins, 2007), 245–46. I have written a book which tries to show this is a seriously mistaken understanding of Scripture, *Jesus: The Only Way to God: Must You Hear the Gospel to Be Saved?* (Grand Rapids, MI: Baker, 2010).

[16] C. S. Lewis, *The Problem of Pain* (New York: Macmillan, 1962), 26–88.

[17] Lewis's view is not simple or completely transparent. He could say, "You will certainly carry out God's purpose, however you act, but it makes a difference to you whether you serve like Judas or like John." Lewis, *Problem of Pain*, 111. And one wonders if by "free will" Lewis sometimes only means "voluntary," rather than "having ultimate self-determination." For example, he writes, "After all, when we are most free, it is only with freedom God has given us; and when our will is most influenced by Grace, it is still *our will*. And if what our will does is not voluntary, and if 'voluntary' does not mean 'free', what are we talking about?" W. H. Lewis and Hooper, *Letters of C. S. Lewis* (1966), 246. And perhaps most significantly, after saying that a fallen soul "could still turn back to God," he adds this

Finally, I should mention that Lewis speaks of the atonement with reverence, but he puts little significance on any of the explanations for how it actually saves sinners. To a Roman Catholic, he wrote in 1941,

> Yes—I think I gave the impression of going further than I intended in saying that all theories of the atonement were "to be rejected if we don't find them helpful." What I meant was "need not be used"—a very different thing. Is there, on your view, any real difference here: that the Divinity of Our Lord has to be believed whether you find it helpful or a "scandal" (otherwise you are not a Christian at all) but the Anselmic theory of Atonement is not in that position. Would you admit that a man was a Christian (and could be a member of your church) who said "I believe that Christ's death redeemed man from sin, but I can make nothing of the theories as to how!" You see, what I wanted to do in these talks was simply to give what is common to us all, and I've been trying to get a *nihil obstat* from friends in various communions. . . . It therefore doesn't much matter how you think of my own theory, because it is advanced only as my own.[18]

These are some of the examples of how Lewis is out of step with Whitefield and Herbert doctrinally. Lewis rarely shows his exegesis. He doesn't deal explicitly with many texts. He is not an expositor. His value is not in his biblical exegesis. It lies elsewhere. And in this chapter, we will see some of what that is.

THE IRONY OF STRENGTHENING MY DOCTRINAL POSITIONS

If you wonder whether Lewis has had a weakening effect on my commitment to the doctrines where we disagree, the answer is: just the

---

footnote: "Theologians will note that I am not here intending to make any contribution to the Pelagian-Augustinian controversy. I mean only that such a return to God was not, even now, an impossibility. Where the initiative lies in any instance of such return is a question on which I am saying nothing." Lewis, *Problem of Pain*, 83. See Douglas Wilson, "Undragoned: C. S. Lewis on the Gift of Salvation," in Piper and Mathis, *Romantic Rationalist*.

[18] W. H. Lewis and Hooper, *Letters of C. S. Lewis* (1966), 197–98. Surely Iain Murray is right to say, "'Substitution' is not one 'theory' of the atonement, it is the heart of the message. This is not the case with Lewis." (Personal correspondence to author, October 10, 2009, quoted with permission.) I think Lewis would have regarded the biblical presentations of justification and reconciliation and propitiation and redemption with greater importance and preciousness if he had attended more carefully the particular texts.

opposite. There was something at the core of his work—his mind—
that had the ironic effect on me of awakening lively affections and firm
convictions that he himself would not have shared.

There was something about the way he read Scripture that made
my own embrace of inerrancy tighter, not looser. There was something
about the way he spoke of grace and God's power that made me value
the particularities of the Reformation more, not less. There was something about the way he portrayed the wonders of the incarnation that
made me more suspicious of his own inclusivism (salvation in other
religions), not less. There was something about the way he spoke of
doctrine as the necessary roadmap that leads to reality,[19] and the way
he esteemed truth and reason and precision of thought, that made me
cherish more, not less, the historic articulations of the biblical explanations of *how* the work of Christ saves sinners—the so-called theories
of the atonement.

LIFE CALLING: DISPLAY AND DEFEND "MERE CHRISTIANITY"

It may be that others have been drawn away by Lewis from these
kinds of convictions and experiences. I doubt that more people, on
the whole, have been weakened in true biblical commitments than
have been strengthened by reading Lewis. Nevertheless, I am sure
it happens. Some, for example, who have taken the road to Roman
Catholicism away from evangelicalism, say Lewis has played a part in
that pilgrimage. He devoted his whole Christian life to defending and
adorning what he called "mere Christianity"—"the Christian religion
as understood *ubique et ab omnibus* [everywhere by everyone]."

> To a layman, it seems obvious that what unites the Evangelical and
> the Anglo-Catholic against the "Liberal" or "Modernist" is some-
> thing very clear and momentous, namely, the fact that both are
> thoroughgoing supernaturalists, who believe in the Creation, the
> Fall, the Incarnation, the Resurrection, the Second Coming, and
> the Four Last Things [death, judgment, heaven, hell]. This unites

---

[19] "For Lewis the doctrines were always absolutely necessary as maps toward one's true destination—
they should never be the *goal* of the Christian life." Jacobs, *The Narnian*, 293.

them not only with one another, but with the Christian religion as understood *ubique et ab omnibus* [everywhere by everyone].

The point of view from which this agreement seems less important than their divisions, or than the gulf which separates both from any non-miraculous version of Christianity, is to me unintelligible. Perhaps the trouble is that as supernaturalists, whether "Low" or "High" Church, thus taken together, they lack a name. May I suggest "Deep Church"; or, if that fails in humility, Baxter's "mere Christians"?[20]

Or, as he says in *The Problem of Pain*, "I have believed myself to be restating ancient and orthodox doctrines. . . . I have tried to assume nothing that is not professed by all baptized and communicating Christians."[21] He believed that when one looks at Christianity across the centuries it has an astounding unity which has great apologetic power.

I myself was first led into reading the Christian Classics, almost accidentally, as a result of my English studies. Some, such as Hooker, Herbert, Traherne, Taylor and Bunyan, I read because they are themselves great English writers; others such as Boethius, St. Augustine, Thomas Aquinas and Dante because they were "influences." . . . They are, you will note, a mixed bag, representative of many Churches, climates and ages. And that brings me to yet another reason for reading them. The divisions of Christendom are undeniable and are by some of these writers most fiercely expressed. But if any man is tempted to think—as one might be tempted who read only contemporaries—that "Christianity" is a word of so many meanings that it means nothing at all, he can learn beyond all doubt, by stepping out of his own century, that this is not so. Measured against the ages "mere Christianity" turns out to be no insipid interdenominational transparency, but something positive, self consistent, and inexhaustible . . .—so unmistakably the same; recognizable, not to be evaded, the odour which is death to us until we allow it to become life. . . .

I know, for I saw it; and well our enemies know it. That unity any of us can find by going out of his own age. . . . You have now got on

---

[20] C. S. Lewis, a letter to R. D. Daunton-Fear, February 8, 1952, in *God in the Dock: Essays on Theology and Ethics*, ed. Walter Hooper (Grand Rapids, MI: Eerdmans, 1970), 336.
[21] Lewis, *Problem of Pain*, 10.

to the great level viaduct which crosses the ages and which looks so high from the valleys, so low from the mountains, so narrow compared to the swamps, and so broad compared to the sheep tracks.[22]

WHAT "MERE CHRISTIANITY" DID NOT MEAN

This means that Lewis rarely tried to distance himself from Roman Catholicism or any other part of Christendom. He rarely spoke about any debates within Christianity itself.[23] But it would be a mistake to take Lewis's focus on "mere Christianity" as a belief that Christian denominations are unnecessary, or that they do not have a valuable place. This is important to see for two reasons. First, some have used his emphasis on "mere Christianity" to discount the theological distinctions among denominations, which Lewis did not do. Second, seeing what he really thought about denominations shows how supremely important doctrinal truth is for him.

In the introduction to *Mere Christianity*, he writes,

I hope no reader will suppose that "mere" Christianity is here put forward as an alternative to the creeds of the existing communions—as if a man could adopt it in preference to Congregationalism or Greek Orthodoxy or anything else. It is more like a hall out of which doors open into several rooms. If I can bring anyone into that hall I shall have done what I attempted. But it is in the rooms, not in the hall, that there are fires and chairs and meals. The hall is a place to wait in, a place from which to try the various doors, not a place to live in. For that purpose the worst of the rooms (whichever that may be) is, I think, preferable. It is true that some people may have to wait in the hall for a considerable time. . . .

You must keep on praying for light: and, of course, even in the hall you must begin trying to obey the rules which are common to the whole house. And above all you must be asking which door is the true one; not which pleases you best by its paint and paneling. In plain language, the question should never be: "Do I like that kind

---

[22] C. S. Lewis, "On the Reading of Old Books," in *God in the Dock*, 203–4.

[23] "I think we must admit that the discussion of these disputed points has no tendency at all to bring outsiders into the Christian fold. . . . Our divisions should never be discussed except in the presence of those who have already come to believe that there is one God and that Jesus Christ is his only son." Lewis quoted in Jacobs, *The Narnian*, 215.

of service?" but "Are these doctrines true: Is holiness here? Does my conscience move me towards this?"

When you have reached your own room, be kind to those who have chosen different doors, and to those who are still in the hall. If they are wrong they need your prayers all the more; and if they are your enemies, then you are under orders to pray for them. That is one of the rules common to the whole house.[24]

Unlike so many ecumenical enthusiasts in his day and ours, Lewis elevated truth to the decisive point: "Above all you must be asking which door is the true one." As you consider which room to live in, ask, above all, "Are these doctrines true?" As your conscience witnesses to that truth, go through that door.

RADICALLY DIFFERENT FROM LIBERALISM

In spite of all Lewis's aberrations from the understanding of salvation that I hold so dear, there was a radical difference between him and most modern liberal theology and postmodern slipperiness. The way he deals with Joy and with absolute truth puts him in another world—a world where I am totally at home, a world where I find both my heart and my mind awakened and made more alive and perceptive and responsive and earnest and hopeful and amazed and passionate for the glory of God. It's this combination of experiencing the stab of God-shaped Joy and defending objective, absolute truth, because of the absolute reality of God, that sets Lewis apart as a rare and wonderful "dinosaur" in the modern world.[25] To my knowledge, there is simply no one else who puts these two things together the way Lewis does.

---

[24] C. S. Lewis, *Mere Christianity* (New York: Macmillan, 1960), xi–xii.

[25] In *"De Descriptione Temporum,"* Lewis's inaugural lecture from the chair of Mediaeval and Renaissance Literature at Cambridge University in 1954, Lewis says,
"I myself belong far more to that Old Western order than to yours. I am going to claim that this, which in one way is a disqualification for my task, is yet in another a qualification. The disqualification is obvious. You don't want to be lectured on Neanderthal Man by a Neanderthaler, still less on dinosaurs by a dinosaur. And yet, is that the whole story? If a live dinosaur dragged its slow length into the laboratory, would we not all look back as we fled? What a chance to know at last how it really moved and looked and smelled and what noises it made! And if the Neanderthaler could talk, then, though his lecturing technique might leave much to be desired, should we not almost certainly learn from him some things about him which the best modern anthropologist could never have told us? He would tell us without knowing he was telling. . . . Ladies and gentlemen, . . . I read as a native text that you must read as foreigners. . . . It is my settled conviction that in order to read Old Western literature aright you must suspend most of the responses and unlearn most of the habits you have acquired in reading modern literature. And because this is the judgment of a native, I claim that, even if the defense of my conviction is weak, the fact of my conviction is a historical datum to which you

MY THESIS IN THIS CHAPTER

My thesis in this chapter is that Lewis's romanticism and his rationalism were the paths on which he came to Christ, and they are the paths
on which he lived his life and did his work. They shaped him into a
teacher and writer with extraordinary gifts for logic and likening—
and evangelism. What I mean by "likening," as we will see, is almost
identical with what I have called *poetic effort* or *dramatic effort* in the
previous chapters. Lewis discovered that joy and reason, longing and
logic, pointed beyond this world, and thus to the deeper meaning of
this world. And he found that this effect of longing and logic (romanticism and rationalism) called forth a kind of language—a poetic effort,
an imaginative use of likening—that illumined the reality of what *is*
by describing it in a way that it is *not*. Thus he spent his life pointing
people, even in his rigorous prose, beyond the world to the meaning
of the world, Jesus Christ.

1. LEWIS THE ROMANTIC

So we will look first at his romanticism and then at his rationality and
how they conspired together to lead him to Christ. Then we will see
how this path led him to see language as a vehicle of this romanticism
and rationalism, and how this led him to be one of the most effective Christian evangelists in the twentieth century. Along with George
Herbert and George Whitefield, Lewis demonstrated that the effort to
speak and write creatively, imaginatively—which I have called *poetic
effort*—was a way of seeing and showing truth and beauty—ultimately
the truth and beauty of God in Christ.

Removing an Old Confusion

In August 1932, Lewis sat down and wrote his first novel in fourteen
days, less than a year after professing faith in Christ.[26] *The Pilgrim's Re-*

---

should give full weight. That way, where I fail as a critic, I may yet be useful as a specimen. I would
even dare to go further. Speaking not only for myself but for all other Old Western men whom you may
meet, I would say, use your specimens while you can. There are not going to be many more dinosaurs."
"Full Text of '*De Descriptione Temporum*,'" *Internet Archive*, accessed October 10, 2013, http://archive.org
/stream/DeDescriptioneTemporum/DeDescriptioneTemporumByC.S.Lewis_djvu.txt.
[26] He wrote to his friend Arthur Greeves, October 1, 1931, "I have just passed on from believing in God
to definitely believing in Christ—in Christianity." Walter Hooper, ed., *The Collected Letters of C. S. Lewis:
Family Letters, 1905–1931*, vol. 1 (San Francisco: HarperSanFrancisco, 2004), 974.

gress is a two-hundred-page allegory of his own pilgrimage to faith in Christ. The subtitle goes like this: "An Allegorical Apology for Christianity, Reason, and Romanticism." So he is defending being a romantic, a rationalist, and a Christian.

But ten years later, when the third edition of the book appeared, he added a ten-page preface to apologize for obscurity and to explain what he means by being a romantic. He said, "The cause for obscurity was the (unintentionally) 'private' meaning I then gave to the word 'Romanticism.'"[27] The word, as he used it, he said, described "the experience which is central in this book."

> What I meant by "Romanticism" . . . and what I would still be taken to mean on the title page of this book—was . . . a particular recurrent experience which dominated my childhood and adolescence and which I hastily called "Romantic" because inanimate nature and marvelous literature were among the things that evoked it.[28]

Romanticism and Stabs of Joy

When we examine his description of the experience he refers to, it turns out to be identical with what ten years later in his autobiography he calls Joy.[29]

> The experience [of romanticism] is one of intense longing. It is distinguished from other longings by two things. In the first place, though the sense of want is acute and even painful, yet the mere wanting is felt to be somehow a delight. . . . This hunger is better than any other fullness; this poverty better than all other wealth.[30]

> There is a peculiar mystery about the *object* of this Desire. Inexperienced people (and inattention leaves some inexperienced all their lives) suppose, when they feel it, that they know what they are

---

[27] C. S. Lewis, *The Pilgrim's Regress* (Grand Rapids, MI: Eerdmans, 1958), 5.
[28] Ibid., 7.
[29] In *Surprised by Joy*, 17–18, Lewis said that this Joy is the experience "of an unsatisfied desire which is itself more desirable than any other satisfaction. I call it Joy, which is here a technical term and must be sharply distinguished both from Happiness and from Pleasure. Joy (in my sense) has indeed one characteristic, and one only, in common with them; the fact that any one who has experienced it will want it again. Apart from that, and considered only in its quality, it might almost equally well be called a particular kind of unhappiness or grief. But then it is the kind we want. I doubt whether anyone who has tasted it would ever, if both were in his power, exchange it for all the pleasures in the world. But then Joy is never in our power and pleasure often is."
[30] Lewis, *Pilgrim's Regress*, 7.

desiring. [Some past event, some perilous ocean, some erotic sug-
gestion, some beautiful meadow, some distant planet, some great
achievement, some quest or great knowledge, etc.]

But every one of these impressions is wrong. The sole merit
I claim for this book is that it is written by one who has proved
them all to be wrong. There is no room for vanity in the claim I
know them to be wrong not by intelligence but by experience. . . .
For I have myself been deluded by every one of these false answers
in turn, and have contemplated each of them earnestly enough to
discover the cheat.[31]

If a man diligently followed this desire, pursuing the false objects
until their falsity appeared and then resolutely abandoning them,
he must come out of last into the clear knowledge that the human
soul was made to enjoy some object that is never fully given—nay,
cannot even be imagined as given—in our present mode of subjec-
tive and spatio-temporal existence.[32]

A Lived Ontological Proof

Lewis called this experience a kind of lived ontological proof of God—
or at least of something beyond the created world. "The dialectic of
Desire," he said, "faithfully followed, would . . . force you not to pro-
pound, but to live through, a sort of ontological proof."[33]

Later when he wrote *Mere Christianity*, he would state it most fa-
mously: "If I find in myself a desire which no experience in this world
can satisfy, the most probable explanation is that I was made for another world."[34]

From Atheism to Christ

So the essence of his romanticism is Lewis's experience of the world that
repeatedly awakened in him a sense that there is always more than this
created world—something other, something beyond the natural world.
At first, he thought the stabbing desire and longing was what he really
wanted. But his conversion to theism and then to Christ would clear

---

[31] Ibid., 8.
[32] Ibid., 10.
[33] Ibid.
[34] Lewis, *Mere Christianity*, 106.

the air and show him what all the longing had been for. God overcame Lewis's atheism in the spring term of 1929. He was thirty years old.

> You must picture me alone in that room in Magdalen, night after night, feeling, whenever my mind lifted even for a second from my work, the steady, unrelenting approach of Him Whom I so earnestly desired not to meet. That which I greatly feared had come upon me. In the Trinity Term of 1929 I gave in, and admitted that God was God, and knelt and prayed: perhaps, that night, the most dejected and reluctant convert in all England. . . . Who can duly adore that love which will open the high gates to a prodigal who is brought in kicking, struggling, resentful, darting his eyes in every direction for a chance of escape?[35]

That was not the end of the struggle. It was two years later, on October 1, 1931, that he wrote to his friend Arthur, "I have just passed on from believing in God to definitely believing in Christ—in Christianity."[36] The great story really is true. God really sent his Son. He really died for our sins. We really can have forgiveness and eternal life in the presence of the One to whom all the Joy was pointing.

The Meaning of Joy: Made for God

Lewis looked back on all his experiences of Joy differently now. Now he knew why the desire was inconsolable and yet pleasant. It was a desire for God. It was evidence that he was made for God.

> The books or the music in which we thought the beauty was located will betray us if we trust to them; it was not *in* them, it only came *through* them, and what came through them was longing. These things—the beauty, the memory of our own past—are good images of what we really desire; but if they are mistaken for the thing itself, they turn into dumb idols, breaking the hearts of their worshipers. For they are not the thing itself; they are only the scent of a flower we have not found, the echo of the tune we have not heard, news from a country we have never yet visited.[37]

---

[35] Lewis, *Surprised by Joy*, 228–29. See Alister McGrath, *C. S. Lewis—A Life* (Carol Stream, IL: Tyndale, 2013), 141–46, for a slight redating of Lewis's conversion to about a year later.
[36] Hooper, *Collected Letters of C. S. Lewis: Family Letters, 1905–1931*, vol. 1, 974.
[37] C. S. Lewis, *The Weight of Glory* (Grand Rapids, MI: Eerdmans, 1949), 4–5.

All his life, he said, "an unattainable ecstasy has hovered just beyond the grasp of [my] consciousness."[38] "The sweetest thing of all my life has been the longing . . . to find the place where all the beauty came from."[39] But when Lewis was born again to see the glory of God in Christ, he never said again that he didn't know where the beauty came from. Now he knew where all the Joy was pointing. On the last page of his autobiography, he explains the difference in his experience of Joy now and before.

> I believe . . . that the old stab, the old bittersweet, has come to me as often and as sharply since my conversion as at any time of my life whatever. But I now know that the experience, considered as a state of my own mind, had never had the kind of importance I once gave it. It was valuable only as a pointer to something other and outer. While that other was in doubt, the pointer naturally loomed large in my thoughts. When we are lost in the woods the sight of the signpost is a great matter. He who first sees it cries, "Look!" The whole party gathers round and stares. But when we have found the road and are passing signposts every few miles, we shall not stop and stare. They will encourage us and we shall be grateful to the authority that set them up. But we shall not stop and stare, or not much; not on this road, though their pillars are of silver and their lettering of gold. "We would be at Jerusalem."[40]

No Less Romantic Joy as a Christian

So Lewis stopped turning Joy into an idol when he found, by grace, that it was "a pointer to something other and outer," namely, to God. Clyde Kilby gave the highest estimation of this theme in Lewis:

> [For Lewis, Joy is] a desire which no natural happiness can ever satisfy, the lifelong pointer toward heaven . . . which gave us such delight and yet are the meager signs of the true rapture He has in heaven for redeemed souls. . . . The culmination of *Sehnsucht* [longing, Joy] in the rhapsodic joy of heaven is, for me at least the strongest single element in Lewis. In one way or other it hovers

---

[38] Lewis, *Problem of Pain*, 148.
[39] Lewis, *Till We Have Faces: A Myth Retold* (New York: Harcourt, 1956), 75.
[40] Lewis, *Surprised by Joy*, 238.

over nearly every one of his books and suggests to me that Lewis's apocalyptic vision is perhaps more real than that of anyone since St. John on Patmos.[41]

This "other and outer" had been wonderful even before he knew that what he was longing for was God. And now that he was a Christian, the piercing longing did not go away just because he knew who it was: "That the old stab, the old bittersweet, has come to me as often and as sharply since my conversion as at any time of my life."

The Central Story of Every Life

Alan Jacobs says, "Nothing was closer to the core of his being than this experience."[42] And Lewis himself says, "In a sense the central story of my life is about nothing else."[43] When you read his repeated descriptions of this experience of romanticism or Joy in *Surprised by Joy* and *Pilgrim's Regress* and *The Problem of Pain* and *The Weight of Glory*, you realize Lewis doesn't see this as a quirk of his personality but as a trait of humanness. All of us are romantics in this sense. Devin Brown says Lewis's "use of the inclusive *you* in these passages . . . makes it clear that Lewis believes this is a longing we have all felt. . . . You might say this is the central story of everyone's life."[44]

For example, in *The Problem of Pain*, Lewis makes the case that even people who think they have never desired heaven don't see things clearly.

> There have been times when I think we do not desire heaven, but more often I find myself wondering whether, in our heart of hearts, we have ever desired anything else . . . tantalizing glimpses, promises never quite fulfilled, echoes that died away just as they caught your ear. But if . . . there ever came an echo that did not die away but swelled into the sound itself—you would know it. Beyond all possibility of doubt you would say, "here at last is the thing I was made for."[45]

---

[41] Clyde S. Kilby, *The Christian World of C. S. Lewis* (Grand Rapids, MI: Eerdmans, 1964), 187.
[42] Jacobs, *The Narnian*, 42.
[43] Lewis, *Surprised by Joy*, 17.
[44] Devin Brown, *A Life Observed: A Spiritual Biography of C. S. Lewis* (Grand Rapids, MI: Brazos, 2013), 5.
[45] Lewis, *Problem of Pain* (New York: Macmillan, 1962), 145–46.

So Lewis saw in his own experience of romanticism the universally human experience. We are all romantics. All of us experience from time to time—some more than others, and some more intensely than others—a longing this world cannot satisfy, a sense that there must be more.

2. LEWIS THE RATIONALIST

We turn now to Lewis's rationalism. And, as with the term *romanticism*, I mean something different from some of its common philosophical uses. All I mean is his profound devotion to being rational—to the principle that there is true rationality and that it is rooted in absolute reason, God's reason.

A Lover of the Law of Noncontradiction

Remember that the subtitle of *The Pilgrim's Regress* is *An Allegorical Apology for Christianity, Reason, and Romanticism*. We've seen what he meant by romanticism. Now what did he mean by reason, and what was his defense of its use?

The simplest way to get at the heart of Lewis's rationality is to say he believed in the law of noncontradiction, and he believed that where this law was abandoned, not only was truth imperiled, but romanticism and Joy were imperiled as well. The law of noncontradiction is simply that contradictory statements cannot both be true at the same time and in the same way.

Lewis saw logic as a real expression of ultimate reality. The laws of logic are not human conventions created differently from culture to culture. They are rooted in the way God is. And these laws of logic make true knowledge of reality possible. "I conclude," he writes, "then that logic is a real insight into the way in which real things have to exist. In other words, the laws of thought are also the laws of things: of things in the remotest space and the remotest time."[46]

Logic as a Parallel Path to God

This commitment to the basic laws of logic, or rationality, led Lewis on the philosophical path to the same Christ that he had found on the

---

[46] C. S. Lewis, "*De Futilitate*" in Walmsley, *C. S. Lewis: Essay Collection*, 674.

path of romanticism or Joy. He put it like this: "This lived dialectic [of my romanticism], and the merely argued dialectic of my philosophical progress, seem to have converged on one goal,"[47] namely, the reality of theism and Christianity and Christ as the Savior of the world.

On the romantic path, Lewis was led again and again to look beyond nature for ultimate reality—finally to God in Christ—because his desires could not be explained as a product of this world. Now how did that same thing happen by the use of his reason?

He looked at the philosophical, scientific cosmology emerging in the modern world and found it self-contradictory.

> If I swallow the scientific cosmology as a whole (that excludes a rational, personal God), then not only can I not fit in Christianity, but I cannot even fit in science. If minds are wholly dependent on brains, and brains on biochemistry, and biochemistry (in the long run) on the meaningless flux of the atoms, I cannot understand how the thought of those minds should have any more significance than the sound of the wind in the trees. And this is to me the final test.[48]

In other words, modern people construct a worldview that treats their thoughts as equivalent to wind in the trees. And then they call these thoughts true. Lewis said that's a contradiction. Atheistic man uses his mind to create a worldview that nullifies the use of his mind.

This is what Lewis meant by the title of his book *The Abolition of Man*. If there is no God as the foundation of logic (like the law of non-contradiction) and the foundation of value judgments (like justice and beauty), then man is abolished. His mind is no more than the rustling of leaves, and his value judgments are no more than ripples on a pond.

> The rebellion of new ideologies against the Tao [the absoluteness of first principles—and ultimately against God] is a rebellion of the branches against the tree: if the rebels could succeed they would find that they had destroyed themselves.[49]

---

47 Lewis, *Pilgrim's Regress*, 10.
48 C. S. Lewis, "Is Theology Poetry?" in Walmsley, *C. S. Lewis: Essay Collection*, 21.
49 C. S. Lewis, *The Abolition of Man* (New York: Macmillan, 1947), 56.

Lewis compares atheistic cosmology to dreaming and Christian theology to being awake. When you are awake you can explain wakefulness and dreaming. But when you are dreaming, you don't have the capacity to explain wakefulness. Similarly:

> Christian theology can fit in science, art, morality, and the sub-Christian religions. The scientific point of view cannot fit in any of these things, not even science itself. I believe in Christianity as I believe that the Sun has risen not only because I see it but because by it I see everything else.[50]

The Path to Closure with Christ

Here's how he describes the way these thoughts brought him on the path of reason to see Christianity as true:

> On these grounds and others like them one is driven to think that whatever else may be true, the popular scientific cosmology at any rate is certainly not. . . . Something like philosophical idealism or Theism must, at the very worst, be less untrue than that. And idealism turned out, when you took it seriously, to be disguised Theism. And once you accepted Theism you could not ignore the claims of Christ. And when you examine them it appeared to be that you could adopt no middle position. Either he was a lunatic or God. And he was not a lunatic.[51]

Truth and Joy, Logic and Longing—Two Paths, One Goal

So we have seen that both Lewis's romanticism and his rationalism brought him to Christ. His lifelong, recurrent experience of the in-breaking of a longing he could not explain by this world led beyond the world to God and finally to Christ. And his lifelong experience of reason and logic led him to see that truth and beauty and justice and science would have no validity at all if there were no transcendent God in whom they were all rooted.

Indeed, the most precious experience of his life—the longing for

---

[50] Lewis, "Is Theology Poetry?" in Walmsley, *C. S. Lewis: Essay Collection*, 21.
[51] Ibid., 20.

God and the finding—would all be empty nothingness if there were no absolute truth and no valid rationality for knowing it.

When Lewis saw the historical Christ and the eternal, objective, absolutely real God as the object of his inconsolable longing (his Joy), he knew that if truth goes, if objective reality goes, if the possibility of knowing goes, if reason goes, then Joy becomes the mirage he feared all his life it might be. Christianity was the end of his quest precisely because it is true. Christ is real. God is real. Truth is real. Here's the way he describes the connection between truth and Joy.

> There was no doubt that Joy was a desire . . . but a desire is turned not to itself but to its object. . . . The form of the desired is in the desire. It is the object which makes the desire harsh or sweet, coarse or choice, "high" or "low." It is the object that makes the desire itself desirable or hateful. I perceived (and this was a wonder of wonders) that just as I had been wrong in supposing that I really desired the Garden of the Hesperides, so also I have been equally wrong in supposing that I desired Joy itself. Joy itself, considered simply as an event in my own mind, turned out to be of no value at all. All the value lay in that of which Joy was the desiring. And that object, quite clearly, was no state of my own mind or body at all.[52]

No Truth, No Joy

Here is the crucial link between truth and Joy. "Joy itself, considered simply as an event in my own mind, turned out to be of no value at all. All the value lay in that of which Joy was the desiring." So we see what is at stake. The entire modern world—and even more so the postmodern world—was moving away from this conviction. Liberal theology, and postmodern cynics who scorn propositions, have gone with the flow of unbelief—subjectivism and relativism. Lewis stood against it with all his might.[53]

---

[52] Lewis, *Surprised by Joy*, 220.
[53] As we have seen, *The Abolition of Man* is Lewis's fury at the purveyors of modern subjectivism in textbooks for young people. He gives this example from one such textbook in his own words. The authors of the textbook refer to a story of Coleridge agreeing with a friend that the beauty of a certain waterfall is *sublime*. The authors comment, "When the man said *That is sublime*, he appeared to be making a remark about the waterfall. . . . Actually . . . he was not making a remark about the waterfall, but a remark about his own feelings. What he was saying was really *I have feelings associate in my mind with the word "Sublime,"* or shortly, *I have sublime feelings*. . . . This confusion is continually present in language

Subjectivism and relativism means "the abolition of man." In the end, it means the destruction of civilization.[54] But long before that, it means the destruction of Joy, because, as Lewis had learned when he became a Christian, an attack on the objective reality of God is an attack on Joy. "Joy itself, considered simply as an event in my own mind, turned out to be of no value at all. All the value lay in that of which Joy was the desiring." All the value lay in God. Without God, the event in my mind called Joy is utterly trivial.

So for Lewis, the experience of Joy and truth, longing and logic, romanticism and rationalism, had conspired to lead him to Christ. And now these two paths would together preserve and deepen his experience of Christ, and would unleash a life of likening—of poetic effort—that would make him one of the most illuminating Christian writers of the twentieth century.

3. Lewis the Master Likener

Therefore, Lewis came to Christ as his Lord and God along the path of *romanticism*, or inconsolable longing, on the one hand, and the path of *rationalism*, or logic, on the other hand. Both of these experiences demanded of him that he own the reality of something beyond this material world, something *other*, something *more* than this world. Both paths finally converged on Jesus Christ as the Creator, and Redeemer, and supreme fulfillment of all our longings, and the ground of all our reasoning.

Both romanticism and rationalism—longing and logic—led him out of this world to find the meaning and validity of this world. This world could not satisfy his deepest desires. And this world could not give validity to his plainest logic. Desires found full and lasting satisfaction and the truth claims of reason found legitimacy in God, not in this world.

Longing and Logic as the Key to Likening

This double experience of romanticism and rationalism, leading finally to God, gave Lewis a key to the power of language to reveal the deeper

---

as we use it. We appear to be saying something very important about something: and actually we are only saying something about our own feelings." Lewis, *Abolition of Man*, 14.
[54] Ibid., 39.

meaning of the world, namely, the key of *likening*. What I mean by the key of likening is this: *Likening some aspect of reality to what it is not can reveal more of what it is.*

God created what is not God. He made not-God the means of revealing and knowing God. And Lewis found the key to what the world really is by being led out of the world to something other than the world, namely, God. He found that this world was most honest and most true when it was pointing beyond itself.

He reasoned like this: if the key to the deepest meaning of this world lies outside this world, then the world will probably be illumined most deeply not simply by describing the world as what it is but by likening the world to what it is not.

Part of what makes Lewis so illuminating on almost everything he touches is his unremitting *rational clarity* and his pervasive use of *likening*. Metaphor, analogy, illustration, simile, poetry, story, myth—all of these are ways of *likening* aspects of reality to what it is *not*, for the sake of showing more deeply what it *is*.

The Paradox of Saying What Is Not to Show What Is

At one level, it seems paradoxical to liken something to what it is *not* in order to show more deeply what it *is*. But that's what life had taught Lewis. And he devoted his whole life to exemplifying and defending this truth. He wrote to T. S. Eliot in 1931 to explain an essay he had sent him and said, "The whole [of it], when completed . . . will re-affirm the romantic doctrine of *imagination as a truth-bearing faculty*, though not quite as the romantics understood it."[55]

Lewis had experienced this all his life—the power of verbal images to illumine reality. But when he became a Christian, this deep-seated way of seeing the world was harnessed for the sake of illumining truth in everything he wrote. In 1954, Lewis sent a list of his books to the Milton Society of America and explained what ties them together like this:

> The imaginative man in me is older, more continuously operative, and that sense more basic than either the religious writer or the

---

[55] Hooper, *Collected Letters of C. S. Lewis: Narnia, Cambridge, and Joy, 1950–1963*, vol. 3, 1523 (emphasis added).

critic. It was he who made me first attempt (with little success) to be a poet. . . . It was he who after my conversion led me to embody my religious belief in symbolical or mythopoeic forms, ranging from *Screwtape* to a kind of theologised sciencefiction. And it was of course he who has brought me, in the last few years, to write the series of Narnian stories for children.[56]

IMAGINATION FOR THE SAKE OF REALITY

He tells us in more than one place why he embraced imaginative literature as such a large part of his calling. All these forms of likening have the paradoxical effect of revealing aspects of the real that we often otherwise miss.

In 1940, he wrote in a letter, "Mythologies . . . are products of imagination in the sense that their content is *imaginative*. The more *imaginative* ones are 'near the mark' in the sense that *they communicate more Reality to us*."[57] In other words, by likening reality to what it is not, we learn more of what it is.

In his essay "On Stories," Lewis comments on the ancient myth of *Oedipus* and says, "It may not be 'like real life' in the superficial sense: but it sets before us an image of what reality may well be like at some more central region."[58]

Lewis calls Tolkien's Lord of the Rings trilogy a "great romance,"[59] and comments in a letter in 1958, "A great romance is like a flower whose smell reminds you of something you can't quite place. . . . I've never met Ents or Elves—but the feel of it, the sense of a huge past, of lowering danger, of heroic tasks achieved by the most apparently unheroic people, of distance, vastness, strangeness, homeliness (all blended together) is so exactly what living feels like to me."[60]

In the preface to *The Pilgrim's Regress*, he comments, "All good allegory exists not to hide but to reveal; to make the inner world more palpable by giving it an (imagined) concrete embodiment."[61] And in his

---

[56] Ibid., 516–17.
[57] Hooper, *Collected Letters of C. S. Lewis: Books, Broadcasts, and War, 1931–1949*, vol. 2, 445 (emphasis added).
[58] C. S. Lewis, "On Stories," in Walmsley, *C. S. Lewis: Essay Collection*, 501.
[59] Hooper, *Collected Letters of C. S. Lewis: Narnia, Cambridge, and Joy, 1950–1963*, vol. 3, 371.
[60] Ibid., 971–72.
[61] Lewis, *Pilgrim's Regress*, 13.

poem "Impenitence," he defends imaginary talking animals by saying that they are

> Masks for Man, cartoons, parodies by Nature
> Formed to reveal us.[62]

In other words, heroic myth, penetrating allegory, great romance, and talking animals are "masks . . . formed to reveal." Again, the paradox of likening—depicting *some aspect of reality as what it is not in order to reveal more of what it is.*

A Likener Everywhere, Not Just in Poems and Stories

But lest I give the wrong impression that Lewis was a likener only in his poetry and fiction, I need to stress that he was a likener every-where—in everything he wrote. Myths and allegories and romances and fairy tales are extended metaphors. But thinking and writing meta-phorically, imaginatively, and analogically were present everywhere in Lewis's life and work.

Lewis was a poet and craftsman and image maker in everything he wrote. Alister McGrath observes that what captivated the reader of Lewis's sermons, essays, and apologetic works, not just his novels, was

> his ability to write prose tinged with a poetic vision, its care-fully crafted phrases lingering in the memory because they have captivated the imagination. The qualities we associate with good poetry—such as an appreciation of the sound of words, rich and suggestive analogies and images, vivid description, and lyrical sense—are found in Lewis's prose.[63]

I think this is exactly right, and it makes him not only refreshing and illuminating to read on almost any topic but also a great model for how to think and write about everything.

Walter Hooper puts it like this:

> A sampling of all Lewis's works will reveal the same man in his poetry as in his clear and sparkling prose. His wonderful imagina-

---

[62] C. S. Lewis, "Impenitence," in *Poems*, ed. Walter Hooper (New York: Harcourt, Brace, and World, 1964), 2.
[63] McGrath, *C. S. Lewis—A Life*, 108.

tion is the guiding thread. It is continuously at work. . . . And this is why, I think, his admirers find it so pleasant to be instructed by him in subjects they have hitherto cared so little for. Everything he touched had his kind of magic about it.[64]

It is indeed pleasant to be instructed by a master likener. Images and analogies and creative illustrations and metaphors and surprising turns of phrase are pleasant. "A word fitly spoken is like apples of gold in a setting of silver" (Proverbs 25:11). Solomon even uses an image to celebrate the pleasure of images. But my point here has not been the *pleasure* of likening but its power of *illumination*, its power to reveal truth.

Lewis's romanticism and his rationalism—his inconsolable longing and his validity-demanding logic—pointed outside the world for the key to understanding the world. And he found that, if the key to the deepest meaning of this world lies outside this world—in its Maker and Redeemer, Jesus Christ—then the world itself will probably be illumined most deeply not simply by describing the world merely as what it is but by *likening* the world to what it's not.

Lewis's unrelenting commitment to *likening*—to the use of images and analogies and metaphor and surprising juxtapositions, even in his most logical demonstrations of truth—was not mainly owing to the greater pleasure it can give but to the deeper truth it can reveal. Lewis loved the truth. He loved objective reality. He believed that the truth of this world and the truth of God could be known. He believed that the use of reason was essential in knowing and defending truth. But he also believed that there are depths of truth and dimensions of reality that *likening* will reveal more deeply than reason.

"Only Supernaturalists Can See Nature"

Unless we see that this world is not ultimate reality but is only like it, we will not see and savor this world for the wonder that it is. Lewis is at his metaphorical best as he explains this with his image-laden prose in this paragraph from *Miracles*.

---

[64] C. S. Lewis, *Poems*, ed. Walter Hooper (New York: Harcourt, Brace & World, 1964), vi.

The Englishness of English is audible only to those who know some other language as well. In the same way and for the same reason, only Supernaturalists really see Nature. You must go a little way from her, and then turn round, and look back. Then at last the true landscape will become visible. You must have tasted, however briefly, the pure water from beyond the world before you can be distinctly conscious of the hot, salty tang of Nature's current. To treat her as God, or as Everything, is to lose the whole pith and pleasure of her [note: pith *and* pleasure]. Come out, look back, and then you will see . . . this astonishing cataract of bears, babies, and bananas: this immoderate deluge of atoms, orchids, oranges, cancers, canaries, fleas, gases, tornadoes, and toads. How could you ever have thought this was the ultimate reality? How could you ever have thought that it was merely a stage-set for the moral drama of men and women? She is herself. Offer her neither worship nor contempt. Meet her and know her. . . . The theologians tell us that she, like ourselves, is to be redeemed. The "vanity" to which she was subjected was her disease, not her essence. She will be cured in character: not tamed (Heaven forbid) nor sterilized. We shall still be able to recognize our old enemy, friend, playfellow and foster-mother, so perfected as to be not less, but more, herself. And that will be a merry meeting.[65]

"Only supernaturalists really see nature." The only people who can know the terrifying wonder of the world are those who know that the world is not the most wonderful and terrifying reality. The world is a likening. The path of romanticism taught Lewis that the world is a likening—the final satisfaction of our longing is not in this world. The path of rationality taught Lewis that the world is a likening. The final validation of our thinking is not in this world. And since this world is a likening—not the goal of our longing or the ground of our logic— therefore it is revealed for what it most profoundly is by likening.

4 . LEWIS THE EVANGELIST

What was Lewis doing in all his works—in all his likening, in all this poetic effort, in all his likening-soaked reasoning? He was pointing. He

---

[65] C. S. Lewis, *Miracles: A Preliminary Study* (New York: Macmillan, 1947), 67–68.

was unveiling. He was depicting the glory of God in the face of Jesus. He was leading people to Christ. The two paths he knew best were the paths of romanticism and rationalism—longing and logic. So these are the paths on which he guided people to Christ.

The Real Business of Life

One of the things that makes him admirable to me, in spite of all our doctrinal differences, is his crystal-clear, unashamed belief that people are lost without Christ and that every Christian should try to win them, including world-class scholars of Medieval and Renaissance literature. And so unlike many tentative, hidden, vague, approval-craving intellectual Christians, Lewis says outright, "The salvation of a single soul is more important that the production or preservation of all the epics and tragedies in the world."[66] And again: "The glory of God, and, as our only means to glorifying Him, the salvation of human souls, is the real business of life."[67]

This is what he was doing in all his likening and all his reasoning. And when Norman Pittenger criticized him in 1958 for being simplistic in his portrayal of Christian faith, Lewis responded in a way that shows us what he was doing in all his work:

> When I began, Christianity came before the great mass of my un-believing fellow-countrymen either in the highly emotional form offered by revivalists or in the unintelligible language of highly cultured clergymen. Most men were reached by neither. My task was therefore simply that of a translator—one turning Christian doctrine, or what he believed to be such, into the vernacular, into language that unscholarly people would attend to and could understand. . . . Dr Pittenger would be a more helpful critic if he advised a cure as well as asserting many diseases. How does he himself do such work? What methods, and with what success, does he employ when he is trying to convert the great mass of storekeepers, lawyers, realtors, morticians, policemen and artisans who surround him in his own city?[68]

---

[66] C. S. Lewis, "Christianity and Literature," in *Christian Reflections* (Grand Rapids, MI: Eerdmans, 1967), 10.
[67] C. S. Lewis, "Christianity and Culture" in *Christian Reflections*, 14.
[68] C. S. Lewis, "Rejoinder to Dr Pittenger," in *God in the Dock*, 183.

Lewis came to Christ on the converging paths of romanticism and rationalism. And as a Christian, he became a master thinker and master likener—a master of poetic effort in story and essay. This is who he was, and this is what he knew. And so this is how he did his evangelism. He bent every romantic effort and every rational effort to help people see what he had seen through his poetic effort—the glory of Jesus Christ, the goal of all his longings, and the solid ground of all his thoughts.

The heavens declare the glory of God,
    and the sky above proclaims his handiwork.
Day to day pours out speech,
    and night to night reveals knowledge.
There is no speech, nor are there words,
    whose voice is not heard. . . .

The law of the Lord is . . .
more to be desired . . . than gold,
    even much fine gold;
sweeter also than honey
    and drippings of the honeycomb.

                Psalm 19:1–3, 7, 10

Oh, taste and see that the Lord is good!

                Psalm 34:8

CONCLUSION

Speak God's Wonders—In His World and in His Word

Seasonable joyousness, honey sweetness, golden fitness, gracious saltiness—such are the descriptions of speech commended in the Bible.

> To make an apt answer is a joy to a man, and a word in season, how good it is! (Proverbs 15:23)

> The wise of heart is called discerning, and sweetness of speech increases persuasiveness. (Proverbs 16:21)

> A word fitly spoken is like apples of gold in a setting of silver. (Proverbs 25:11)

> Let your speech always be gracious, seasoned with salt. (Colossians 4:6)

Of course, there are many other descriptions of good speech, such as truth (Ephesians 4:15), clarity (Colossians 4:4), boldness (Ephesians 6:20), sincerity (2 Corinthians 2:17), in the name of the Lord Jesus (Colossians 3:17). But our focus in this book has been on joyful, honey-like, strikingly fitting, salty language. I have called the mental, emotional, prayerful, God-dependent, self-humbling, Christ-exalting exertion it takes to find and express these words *poetic effort*.

The aim has not been to suggest that all Christians write poems (though I suspect we all will someday). Poetic effort is not the effort to write poems. Poetic effort is the effort to see and savor and speak the wonder—the divine glory—that is present everywhere in the world God made, in the history God guides, and in the Word God inspired.

THE CENTRAL FOCUS OF THIS BOOK

The particular focus we have circled back to frequently is the insight that the effort to say beautifully is a way of also seeing beauty. By *beautifully*, I don't mean flowery or ostentatious or ornate or showy or elevated. I mean illuminating, well-timed, penetrating, creative, fresh, imaginative, striking, awakening, provocative—while not being trite, clichéd, clever, cute, silly, obtrusive, awkward, puerile, faddish, corny, or boring. The very fact that so many words exist to describe poorly chosen words shows how common they are. I am pleading for us to do better.

So the central point of this book—saying beautifully is a way of seeing beauty—doesn't mean let's all create poems or let's all be artsy. It means that as you try to find words that seem worthy of the worth of what you have seen, the worth of what you have seen becomes clearer and deeper. That's the point.

The point is to waken us to go beyond the common awareness that using worthy words helps others feel the worth of what we have seen. Everybody knows that. It is a crucial and wise insight. And love surely leads us to it. But I am going beyond that. Or under that. Or before it. The point of this book has been that finding worthy words for worthy discoveries not only helps others feel their worth but also helps us feel the worth of our own discoveries. Groping for awakening words in the darkness of our own dullness can suddenly flip a switch and shed light all around what it is that we are trying to describe—and feel. Taking hold of a fresh word for old truth can become a fresh grasp of the truth itself. Telling of beauty in new words becomes a way of tasting more of the beauty itself.

GEORGE HERBERT

George Herbert and C. S. Lewis virtually said this point explicitly. Why did Herbert labor to find extraordinary words and unprecedented ways of describing the glories of the love of Christ?

> [Poetry] is no office, art, or news,
> Nor the Exchange, or busie Hall;

> But it is that which while I use
> I am with thee. . . .[1]

The very effort to find the words for Christ brought him closer to Christ. It opened the treasure chest of redeeming love. Yes, his poems illumine us. But first they illumined Herbert. He did not merely find the sweetness of Christ and then create words so we could taste. No. The creating of the words was part of finding the sweetness. He tasted Christ by means of the poetic effort to tell well.

GEORGE WHITEFIELD

George Whitefield wrote little and preached almost ceaselessly—sometimes as much at sixty hours in a week. He did not reflect theoretically on his way of speaking. But from what he said, and what others experienced, we know that his verbal and theatrical poetic effort was a way of feeling and heralding the greatest realities in the world. This story is worth repeating:

> I'll tell you a story [Whitefield said]. One day the Archbishop . . . said to Butterton [a famous actor] . . . "Pray inform me Mr. Butterton, what is the reason you actors on stage can affect your congregations with speaking of things imaginary, as if they were real, while we in church speak of things real, which our congregations only receive as if they were imaginary?" "Why my Lord," says Butterton, "the reason is very plain. We actors on stage speak of things imaginary, as if they were real and you in the pulpit speak of things real as if they were imaginary." Therefore, I will bawl [shout loudly], I will not be a velvet-mouthed preacher.[2]

We may readily admit that in one sense Whitefield was "acting" as he preached. That is, he was taking the part of the characters in the drama of his sermons and pouring all his energy—his poetic effort—into making their parts real. And this poetic effort was not only for his listeners but for himself. The key words in the story above are "as if."

---

[1] George Herbert, "The Quidditie" in Helen Wilcox, ed., *The English Poems of George Herbert* (Cambridge: Cambridge University Press, 2007), 254.
[2] Harry S. Stout, *The Divine Dramatist: George Whitefield and the Rise of Modern Evangelicalism* (Grand Rapids, MI: Eerdmans, 1991), 239–40.

"We actors on stage speak of things imaginary, *as if* they were real and you in the pulpit speak of things real *as if* they were imaginary." White-field resolved to do neither. He would speak of things real *as if* they were real, because they *are* real. This "as if" is what I mean by poetic effort. It gropes not for words to make the unreal real but for words to see and savor and speak the real as real. The true as true. The glorious as glorious. The horrible as horrible. The tender as tender. The tough as tough. The joyful as joyful. And reaching for a voice that matches the truth—this is my point—wakens the speaker as well as the hearer.

C. S. LEWIS

C. S. Lewis came to faith in Christ by learning that this world, for all its wonders and joys, is not what his heart was finally made for. All the joys of nature and literature were pointing to something—"something other and outer." God had revealed himself in terms of what he was not. The world and everything in it was a creative language pointing to the real thing. Which also meant that the realness of the world could only be known, in its true depth and beauty, by those who know that it is not everything.

> Only Supernaturalists really see Nature. You must go a little way from her, and then turn round, and look back. Then at last the true landscape will become visible. You must have tasted, however briefly, the pure water from beyond the world before you can be distinctly conscious of the hot, salty tang of Nature's current.[3]

So to truly know God, we must attend to what he has made—the world, the written Word, the flesh of the incarnate Son. And to know what he has made, we must attend to God. From this, Lewis drew out his understanding of myth and story and metaphor and poetry—and poetic effort. He saw that one can speak deeply and truly of God and this world only by reaching for the terms of the other—God in terms of the world, the world in terms of God. The world is not what it is without God, and God is not known for who he is except through the world. But this implied something else. Lewis also saw that one can

---

[3] C. S. Lewis, *Miracles: A Preliminary Study* (New York: Macmillan, 1947), 67.

see the world and God deeply and truly only by reaching for the terms of the other. We don't just *speak* the world and God truly by stretching for the words outside the world and outside God, but we also *see* the world and God that way. We would not see them for what they are if we did not try to think them and speak them in the terms of the other.

Thus Lewis provides us with a deeper foundation for the point of this book. Saying beautifully as way of seeing beauty—saying surprisingly and imaginatively, speaking in terms of "the other"—is rooted in the fact that God and nature are "other" from each other. Nature is not what it is apart from "the other" (God), and God is not known for what he is apart from "the other" (the world he made). This foundational truth trickles all the way down to our everyday speech. The words "just as" and "like" and "as if" are echoes of this foundational truth. We see more of what *is* when we describe it in terms of what it *is not*.

BENEDICTION

May the Lord Jesus himself protect us from self-exalting, Christ-obscuring eloquence. But may he grant us a humble, Christ-exalting poetic habit of speaking his wonders—from the simplest in his world to the greatest in his Word—in words of seasonable joyousness, honey sweetness, golden fitness, and gracious saltiness. May he do it so that we ourselves might first taste, then tell.

INDEX OF SCRIPTURES

Index of Persons

INDEX OF SUBJECTS

desiringGod

If you would like to explore further the vision of God and life presented in this book, we at Desiring God would love to serve you. We have thousands of resources to help you grow in your passion for Jesus Christ and help you spread that passion to others. At desiringGod.org, you'll find almost everything John Piper has written and preached, including more than sixty books. We've made over thirty years of his sermons available free online for you to read, listen to, download, and watch.

In addition, you can access hundreds of articles, find out where John Piper is speaking, and learn about our conferences. Desiring God has a whatever-you-can-afford policy, designed for individuals with limited discretionary funds. If you'd like more information about this policy, please contact us at the address or phone number below. We exist to help you treasure Jesus and his gospel above all things because *he is most glorified in you when you are most satisfied in him*. Let us know how we can serve you!

Desiring God

Post Office Box 2901 / Minneapolis, Minnesota 55402
888.346.4700 mail@desiringGod.org

Each book in The Swans Are Not Silent series focuses
on three renowned leaders from church history,
offering a close look at the course of their individual
lives and their impact on our own spirituality today.

THE LEGACY OF SOVEREIGN JOY
Augustine, Martin Luther, John Calvin

THE HIDDEN SMILE OF GOD
John Bunyan, William Cowper, David Brainerd

THE ROOTS OF ENDURANCE
John Newton, Charles Simeon, William Wilberforce

CONTENDING FOR OUR ALL
Athanasius, John Owen, J. Gresham Machen

FILLING UP THE AFFLICTIONS OF CHRIST
William Tyndale, Adoniram Judson, John Paton

Visit crossway.org for more information.